MARCO POLO

CHANNEL ISLANDS

with Local Tips
*The author's special recommendations are
highlighted in yellow throughout this guide*

There are five symbols to help you find your way around this guide:

Marco Polo's top recommendations – the best in each category

sites with a scenic view

places where the local people meet

places where young people get together

(104/A1)
pages and coordinates for the Road Atlas of the Channel Islands
(U/A1) *coordinates for the City Maps St Helier and St Peter Port
inside back cover*
(O) *area not covered by maps*

MARCO ⊕ POLO

Travel guides and language guides in this series:

Alaska • Algarve • Amsterdam • Australia/Sydney • Bahamas • Barbados
Berlin • Brittany • California • Canada • Channel Islands • Costa
Brava/Barcelona • Costa del Sol/Granada • Côte d'Azur • Crete • Cuba
Cyprus • Dominican Republic • Eastern Canada • Eastern USA • Florence
Florida • Gran Canaria • Greek Islands/Aegean • Ibiza/Formentera • Ireland
Istanbul • Lanzarote • London • Mallorca • Malta • Mexico • New York
New Zealand • Normandy • Paris • Prague • Rhodes • Rome • San Francisco
Scotland • South Africa • Southwestern USA • Tenerife • Turkish Coast
Tuscany • USA: Southern States • Venice • Western Canada

French • German • Italian • Spanish

Marco Polo would be very interested to hear your
comments and suggestions. Please write to:

North America:
Marco Polo North America
70 Bloor Street East
Oshawa, Ontario, Canada
(B) 905-436-2525

United Kingdom:
GeoCenter International Ltd
The Viables Centre
Harrow Way
Basingstoke, Hants RG22 4BJ

Our authors have done their research very carefully, but should any errors or omissions
have occurred, the publisher cannot be held responsible for any injury, damage
or inconvenience suffered due to incorrect information in this guide

Cover photograph: Jersey, Gorey and Mont Orgueil Castle (Schapowalow: Huber)
Photos: Amberg: Schraml (18, 37, 41); author (22, 25, 26, 31, 44, 75, 96);
Irek (4, 7, 12, 16, 50, 52, 59, 63, 66, 69, 80, 83, 84, 87); Janicke (32, 57, 77, 88, 90);
Mauritius: Feature Pix (28); Hubatka (103); Silvestris: Stadler (11, 15, 36, 38, 70, 73)

2nd revised edition 2000
© Mairs Geographischer Verlag, Ostfildern, Germany
Author: Hans-Peter Reiser
Translator: Jane Riester
English edition 2000: Gaia Text
Editorial director: Ferdinand Ranft
Chief editor: Marion Zorn
Cartography for the Road Atlas: © Mairs Geographischer Verlag
Design and layout: Thienhaus/Wippermann
Printed in Germany

CONTENTS

Discover the Channel Islands!

A happy blend of the sometimes eccentric British way of life and the charm of French savoir-vivre

When asked what he liked about the Channel Islands, the French writer Victor Hugo answered: 'I love everything'. This simple statement summed up his relationship with the islands, which he developed during his long period of enforced exile. It was this affinity that helped him to endure the bitterness undoubtedly caused by his prolonged separation from his beloved Paris. No place is more French in character than the small group of English islands that lie off the Normandy coast. This is doubtless owing both to the proximity of France and to the centuries-old ties that link the islands to their closest neighbour. This connection with France is expressed most clearly in the happy marriage of traditional, on occasion somewhat eccentric British lifestyle and the charming, French savoir-vivre. To this day, this dominant feature, so characteristic of the islands, can be observed in many aspects of island life and in the

Portelet Bay in Jersey

personalities of their inhabitants. And no one seems to mind in the slightest. On the contrary, everyone who comes here enjoys the Channel Islands for what they are and would not change them for the world. Victor Hugo must certainly have felt this way too, which makes his declaration of love for the islands all the more credible.

Undoubtedly, the five Channel Islands have their own distinct character, despite their common topography. They were formerly all part of the Cotentin peninsula. Around 8,000 BC, the rising sea-level, brought about by the melting of the ice sheets at the end of the last Ice Age, finally severed all physical links with the European continent. The two largest islands, Jersey and Guernsey, plus the smaller Alderney, Sark and Herm, came into existence as a result. They are surrounded by numerous smaller islands – some not much more than large rocks – which remain largely uninhabited to this day. The obvious strategic importance of the islands in the English Channel has been fundamental to their development and history.

As early as the Bronze Age, the islands were important stops on the trade route along the Atlantic coast. In the Iron Age that followed, fortifications were erected by the Celtic settlers to protect themselves against invasion from neighbouring countries. This didn't stop the Romans from seizing the islands, around the time of Christ's birth, and using them as a base for their Channel fleet and as a trading centre. Back under Celtic control from the fourth century AD onwards, the islands were not only the subject of the benevolent attention of Breton missionaries, but also a target for the less-than-friendly Germanic pirates. Two of those missionaries, Brelade and Helier – subsequently sanctified – together with Sampson, Magloire and Vignalis brought Christianity to the islands at about this time.

Things began to heat up around the start of the ninth century, when the Vikings embarked on their *Tour de France* and settled in the Seine delta, soon to become known as the Normans. Their leader, Rollo, rose to become Duke of Normandy, and the quarrelling over the islands began. His son and heir, William Longsword, stepped in and captured the islands in 933, placing them under Norman rule. In 1066, William the Conquerer defeated the English at the Battle of Hastings and crowned himself King of England. Henceforth, until the beginning of the 14th century, the islands were under Anglo-Norman control. The islands changed hands several times during the Hundred Years' War (1339–1453), fought between France and England, who regarded them as fair game. In 1468, they were finally ceded to the English Crown and remained in English hands – barring the occasional skirmish in the years in between – until the present day. The only, tragic interruption came with the five-year German occupation during World War II.

Officially, then, the islands have not been French for over 500 years. Their inner bond with France has lived on, however, as demonstrated by the fact that the monarch in London is not recognized as King or Queen of England, but only as the Duke of Normandy. *Le Grand Coutumier*, a law introduced in the 13th century, forms the basis of the current legal system. A curious feature of this system is the *Clameur de Haro*. Then, as now, an injured party may, during a dispute, call out 'Haro, Haro, à l'aide mon Prince, on me fait tort!' ('Haro, Haro, help me, my Prince. They do me wrong!'), adding the Lord's Prayer in French, thus suspending the matter until it can be settled in court.

Lying peacefully together in the English Channel, the islands appear to form a single political unit, and, because they are British, would seem to belong to the United Kingdom. Appearances can, however, be deceptive. They are neither part of Great Britain nor of the European Union, and they exercise extensive autonomy in domestic affairs. They are not even a unified state in themselves: each island is independent. The four largest islands each have their own parliament and legal system, they issue their own coinage, postage stamps and telephone cards and they are empowered to levy taxes. Retail prices vary, too, from island to island. There are no political parties, or professional politicians, no parliamentary allowances or special privileges. All public offices are honorary positions.

Until the end of the 15th century, the islands were governed jointly on behalf of the English king by a *Governor*. In 1470, the creation of two *Bailiwicks*, each presided over by its own governor, effectively separated the islands, a situation that still exists today. The *Bailiwick of Jersey* is a political unit on its own; Guernsey, Alderney, Sark and Herm constitute the *Bailiwick of Guernsey*, whereby each island is determined to preserve its own identity at all costs.

Taking all this into account, you wonder how the islands came to be labelled *British*. Naturally, links to Britain are close; just as the monarchy serves to cement traditional historical bonds, so has common sense dictated numerous mutually beneficial arrangements. Hence, the British government is responsible for foreign defence and monetary policy on the islands and, in addition, the *Privy Council*, a British crown council, oversees all laws passed by the island parliaments. This is as far as British rule goes.

Since Britain directs monetary policy on the islands, the value of the island currency is tied to that of the pound sterling. The Channel Islands have passed their own laws, facilitating the creation of a tax haven of international importance. They offer excellent conditions for investment, enticing clients from Britain and overseas. There is, for example, no value added tax,

A favourite amongst photographers: Apple Cottage in Rozel on Jersey

History at a glance

6000–4000 BC
Dolmens, standing stones and other relics are erected by early settlers

2600 BC
Megalithic passage grave at La Hougue Bie on Jersey

1000 BC
Burial mound at Hougue Fouque on Guernsey

500 BC
Settlements and fortifications on Alderney

56 BC
The Romans occupy Celtic Gaul and the islands

AD 500–850
Islands' conversion to Christianity by St Helier, St Sampson and St Magloire

933
Duke William captures the Channel Islands for Normandy

1066
William the Conquerer wins at Hastings and is crowned King of England

1087
Robert inherits Normandy and the Channel Islands

1106
His brother, King Henry I, defeats Robert and wins back Normandy and the Channel Islands for England

1204
King John loses Normandy to France, but retains the Channel Islands

1339–1468
France conquers and rules the Channel Islands

1569
The islands, part of the diocese of Coutances, are ceded to the Church of England

1642–46
Islands become embroiled in the English Civil War

1781
The French take Jersey briefly at the Battle of Jersey

1852
French writer Victor Hugo spends 18 years of his exile on Jersey and on Guernsey

1870
First railway line built on Jersey. In 1879, Guernsey follows suit

1902
The Battle of Flowers held for the first time on Jersey

1935
First airport on Alderney, on Jersey in 1937, and on Guernsey two years later

1940–45
Occupation by German troops

1969
Jersey and Guernsey issue their own postage stamps, Alderney does the same in 1983

a low level of income tax, a high degree of confidentiality in banking affairs and various other tax concessions. More than one hundred banks and insurance companies from all over the world have established branches on the islands, engaged in healthy competition for investor's money. Consequently, many billions of pounds lie deposited here, out of reach of domestic tax men – and the amount is increasing daily.

The financial sector has boomed to such an extent that it has overtaken traditional economic activities to become the most important source of income for the islanders. In turn, new career opportunities have opened up. Young people in particular were eager to take on these lucrative jobs and – if their expensive-looking cars are anything to go by – have achieved great success. Traditional jobs were left to foreigners. The old, somewhat dull image of the islands has become more colourful, more international – and their new look suits them.

Approaching Jersey and Guernsey from the air, visitors are amazed at the number of greenhouses, which seem to cover the islands with a gleaming cloak. Once on solid ground, you'll find they are relatively unobtrusive, unless, of course, you go looking for them. When you take into consideration the millions of cut flowers produced here, it is clear that the agriculture industry is still keen to play a major role in the islands' economies. Roses, carnations, iris, amongst others, are exported in large quantities to Great Britain and the continent. The same applies to the *Jersey Royal*, the ever-popular variety of early potato, and the *Guernsey Tom*, a delicious type of tomato, both mainstays of the export market. Not forgetting, of course, strawberries and kiwi fruit.

The dairy industry is still of major – although diminishing – importance. The brown Jersey and Guernsey cows, as well as being extremely photogenic against the background of their lush green pastures, give excellent milk. This is transformed in the dairies into various types of milk, butter and cheese and the islanders' beloved cream. We recommend you try a delicious cream tea – for many visitors, it becomes an almost daily ritual.

Although finance is undoubtedly the biggest contributor to the well-being of the islands, tourism remains an important branch of the economy. The reputation the islands have established for themselves as a holiday paradise should not only be maintained, but continuously built upon. By their very nature, the islands are in an ideal position to do so.

Torn away from the continent, the islands lie in the English Channel, basking in the warm currents of the Gulf Stream. This guarantees adequate rainfall and favourable temperatures all year round, which, in turn, enable the survival of the lush and sometimes exotic vegetation. In the spring, subtropical plants transform the palm-fringed parks and gardens into a sea of flowers. The open country, too, holds many delights for plant-lovers, such as a walk down densely wooded mill valleys into the heart of the island or along cliff-top paths edged with ferns and gorse in search of the coastal beauty spots. This really is nature at her finest.

The best way to explore the islands is on foot or by bicycle, especially when venturing off the beaten track. The few touristic highlights are quickly reached by car, since the three largest islands boast a dense road network. Admittedly, the road signs in some cases leave a lot to be desired. It is, therefore, quite possible to get lost when trying to reach a particular destination. The roads, lined with high stone walls and hedges, are often very narrow, which, together with the necessity of driving on the left, present quite a challenge to some North American or Canadian visitors. All in all, driving on the Channel Islands is not always an unmitigated pleasure. Those who prefer to play it safe can always fall back on the reliable bus services on Jersey and Guernsey.

Whichever natural feature you have chosen for a visit, it's bound to lie somewhere on a scale between 'exciting' and 'spectacular'. This is largely on account of the inclination of the island terrain. With the exception of Sark, the islands slope from steep cliffs on one side gently down to the flat coastline on the other. Here, you'll find seemingly endless sandy beaches, whereas the cliffs are characterized by bizarre rock formations and delightful bays for swimming and sunbathing. The tidal range – here almost 14 m – means that the beaches and bays are in a permanent state of flux. What looks, at low tide, like an ideal place to swim, may have vanished once the tide has come in only a few hours later. Boat trips, bathing excursions and coastal walks are not without their dangers, and it is strongly recommended that you carry a copy of the tide tables with you – and use it. Only then can you be sure of not getting carried away by the strong currents or finding your route back to dry land cut off suddenly. This warning is not intended to alarm, however. Here, as anywhere else, the old saying applies: 'It's better to be safe than sorry.'

Having said all this, however, the beauty of the Channel Islands should not blind us to their less attractive aspects. It's easy to get carried away when describing the magnificent medieval fortifications and towers. On the other hand, faced with this century's monstrous concrete eyesores, the visitor is shocked and dismayed. These remnants of the German Occupation, part of the Atlantic defence cordon, cannot be removed and must somehow be tolerated. Local residents have resigned themselves to this fact. Many bunkers now house museums, packed with relics of that unfortunate period. Some are even used to host parties. Others exist purely as monuments. Happily, though, no grudge is harboured against German holidaymakers.

Guests are given a warm welcome on all the islands. The residents are friendly and hospitable. Their cosmopolitan atti-

Victor Hugo, St Peter Port, Guernsey

claim. The visitor can only profit from this.

Victor Hugo visited and came to love all the islands. You, too, need not restrict yourself to one island when planning your holiday; your trip can easily include two or three. On the face of it, the islands appear the same, and although they are so close together, they are all different. Each one is beautiful in its own way and has its own character. It is quite possible to see the Channel Islands in two weeks. Four days in Jersey, two in Alderney and six in Guernsey, including day trips to Herm and Sark: all in all, that's two weeks, including the journey to and from the islands. If you can afford a third week just to relax, you could take the time to spend it on the island you liked best the first time round. The islands are small – even Jersey, the largest – and all touristic highlights are within quick and easy reach. That leaves plenty of time to bathe on long, sandy beaches or in secluded coves and walk along cliff-top paths or in the idyllic island heart.

The islands are linked chiefly by ship. A regular ferry service connects Jersey and Guernsey. Sark can be reached by boat from both larger islands; Herm, on the other hand, only from Guernsey. To reach Alderney, you must fly from Jersey or Guernsey, since there is no regular ferry service. Flights also join the two island capitals. 'Island hopping' is no problem, as you can see. All you have to do is decide on which of these beautiful islands your holiday should begin.

tude stems from their profound self-confidence. Rather than criticize a foreigner, they are more likely to poke fun at their island neighbours. The people of Jersey are seen as being over zealous, *nouveau riche* and showy. Guernsey residents are, on the other hand, quite the opposite: middle-class and narrow-minded. Alderney is even branded as the home of the heavy drinkers. These jibes are not meant to be taken seriously, as is clear from the label attached to the people of Alderney. This refers less to the amount of alcohol consumed, as to the liberal opening hours of the island's pubs. Maybe the other islanders are just envious? The healthy rivalry between Jersey and Guernsey goes back a long way. Each island vies with the other as the more attractive holiday destination, and no effort is spared to justify this

From high and low tide to walking

All you need to know about the Channel Islands, past and present

High and low tide

The seas around the Channel Islands constitute the northern end of the Gulf of St Malo. Consequently, the islands are exposed to a tidal range unparalleled in the rest of Europe. The difference between high and low tide can be as much as 14 m. The islands, with the exception of Sark, are characterized by both flat, sandy beaches and steep, jagged cliffs, in equal proportions. Consequently, the ebb and flow of the water makes for an ever-changing picture. Low tide exposes endless, wide beaches and pretty coves between the cliffs and headlands. The countless rocks and reefs that materialize at the same time explain the islands' grim reputation amongst seafarers. High tide conceals these bathing attractions once more, the sea water submerging beaches and bays and transforming the landscape completely. Clearly, more adventurous holidaymakers can – even unwittingly – put themselves at great risk, given such conditions. Many of the coastal attractions are accessible only at low tide. If you fail to take into account the incredible speed with which ebb and flow succeed each other, you could be putting your life in danger. Take a tip from the sailors who ply the waters around the islands: take care and be sure to consult the tide tables when planning trips to the coast!

Flora and fauna

The Gulf Stream, which warms the English Channel, plus 2,000 hours of sunshine per year combine to give the Channel Islands a mild, Mediterranean climate, suitable for many exotic plants. In the dunes, on the cliffs, in gardens and in the meadows, something is sure to be in full bloom – all year round. Whether growing wild or carefully nurtured, an endless variety of flowers and plants has established itself over the centuries: primula, narcissus, hyacinth, orchid, tamarisk, sloe, heather, sea holly, not forgetting rose, rhododendron, azalea, hydrangea, to name but a few. Palm, ash, pine and

Accessible only at low tide: Corbière Lighthouse on Jersey

evergreen oak grow in parks and woods. This enormous diversity of plant life attracts numerous animals. Many species of bird have made themselves at home here, making the Channel Islands an eldorado for ornithologists and bird-lovers. Spring and autumn see the arrival of migratory birds, while songbirds, such as wren and blackcap, and woodland birds, such as woodpecker and stonechat, are permanent residents. You can observe many seabirds in the dunes and on the beaches, in particular seagulls and terns, but also cormorants and gannets. The magnificent and diverse range of plants and animals complements the natural beauty of the islands.

Sacred cows

When talking of *sacred cows*, we usually think of India or Pakistan. Here, on the Channel Islands, the Jersey and Guernsey cows enjoy a similar status: the islanders love their cattle. And rightly so. They are not only pleasing to look at, they are of the finest pure-bred stock. Pedigree documents verify that the ancestors of today's cows and bulls can be traced back over 100 years. Since the import of livestock was prohibited during this period, the pure breeding of the islands' cattle is guaranteed. Highly priced around the world, the export of these extremely productive animals has always made an important contribution to the prosperity of the islands. After all, the average price for a cow stands at around £1,000, top-quality animals can even fetch £3,000. Today, the bovine beauties graze the lush pastures

chiefly to make milk, for which islander would readily do without that incomparable cream?

Victor Hugo

Throughout the centuries, a substantial number of asylum-seekers have sought and found refuge on the Channel Islands. Amongst them were several famous names, such as *Victor Hugo*, the French writer who was forced to leave France suddenly in 1851. Following Napoleon III's coup d'état, Hugo was threatened with arrest for his republican sentiments. His flight took him via Brussels and Antwerp to London. To be closer to his beloved France, however, he left Southampton in 1852 for Jersey. Together with numerous other *proscrits*, he used the newspaper *L'Homme* as a vehicle to agitate the despised Emperor in Paris. When, in 1854, during the Crimean War, *Queen Victoria* joined forces with *Napoleon III*, Hugo extended his criticism to include the English royal family. Royalist Jersey deported the *proscrits* and Victor Hugo followed them to Guernsey, where he then settled down. Some years later, he bought *Hauteville House*, high above the harbour of *St Peter Port*, and bequeathed it finally to the city of Paris. Today, it houses the Victor Hugo museum.

During this period in exile, Victor Hugo wrote both novels *Les Misérables* (1862) and *Les Travailleurs de la Mer* (1866), which, together with *Notre-Dame de Paris* (1831), completed his famous trilogy. *Les Travailleurs de la Mer* is the only one of Hugo's novels that is set in Guernsey. Many of the places described in the novel are fictional, others can be traced even today. The final novel Hugo wrote in Guernsey was *L'Homme qui rit* (1869), a fitting description of the author himself, perhaps, on his return to Paris in 1870 and on reflection of the happy time he spent on the Channel Islands.

Jersey Lily

To this day, Lillie Langtry, daughter of a parish priest from St Saviour, is revered in Jersey as an almost legendary figure. Her beauty was unsurpassed – and she knew how to use it to her advantage! Writers, artists and other members of fashionable society were at her beck and call, as she took London by storm. John E. Millais immortalized her in a painting in which she is shown holding a lily, giving rise to her epithet 'Jersey Lily'. Oscar Wilde was an ardent admirer and dedicated lovesick poems to her. He introduced her to the theatre, where she soon caused a sensation, rivalling that other great star, Sarah Bernhardt. Having a good head for business and the ability to market her image well, she toured America, acccompanied by a theatre group, where she scored one success after another. Her fairy-tale career over, she died in 1929, aged 76, in Monte Carlo, and was buried in St Saviour.

Climate

As a rule, you can count on the island summers being not too hot and the winters not too cold. Average temperatures lie

Pure-bred Guernsey cows: world famous for their delicious cream

between 9°C (48°F) and 20°C (68°F). The Channel Islands owe their year-round mild climate to the warm waters of the Gulf Stream that envelop them. The water temperature rises to a maximum of 16°C (61°F) (in high summer, along the wide open beaches, somewhat higher) and has an unpredictable effect on the weather. In the cooler time of the year, the high humidity can lead to a build-up of fog, which is quickly dispersed by the strong sea breezes. Continuous rain is rare, as are extended periods of fine weather. Below-average annual rainfall (880 mm per year) and an above-average number of sunshine hours (2,000 hours per year) mean that it's wise to pack your holiday suitcase for all eventualities.

Last orders, please!

It's a well-known fact that the islanders are freedom-loving people, but they can also be austere, almost puritanical. Men, of all people, bear the brunt of this – down at the pub! Sunday finds them searching in vain for their *pint*. And, on top of that, drinks are served only together with a meal. Publicans are compelled to uphold the islands' strict licensing laws. These categorically state that a visit to the bar must satisfy the hunger as well as quench the thirst. Admittedly, a small snack is sufficient as an alibi. Then you're free to drink whatever you want and as much as you want. The only time limit is determined by the landlord, just before closing time, when he calls out 'Last orders, please!'

Old Portelet Inn on Jersey has been popular for centuries

Artists

The Channel Islands were not only a magnet for writers – such as *François René de Chateaubriand* (1768–1848) and *Victor Hugo* (1802–85) – artists, too, were attracted by their particular charm. Englishman *William Turner* (1745–1851), a successful painter of land- and seascapes, came in 1829 and was much impressed by the coastline of Sark. Jersey-born painter *John Everett Millais* (1829–96) spent his early years here before rising to fame – and a knighthood – in London. His portrait of the 'Jersey Lily' can be seen in the Jersey Museum. French Impressionist *Pierre-Auguste Renoir* (1841–1919) succumbed, in 1883, not only to the natural beauty of the beaches and cliffs, but also to the feminine charms of those who adorned them! In all, he produced 18 works on Jersey and Guernsey, amongst them the famous *Au Bord de la Mer.*

Martello towers

During centuries of conflict between England and France, the unfortunate role of advance guard always fell to the Channel Islands. French troops posed a constant threat, not least because the long, flat beaches and secluded coves were ideal landing places for invaders. In 1778, construction work began on 31 fortified towers, which were supplemented, in 1781 following a French raid, by further round defence towers to strengthen weak spots on the coast. These latter towers were of identical design, with a diameter of 12 m and a height of 10 m. The entrance was high above the ground and could be reached only by using a rope-ladder. The lower chamber was used as an ammunition store, the upper chamber as living quarters for the usually ten-man garrison. A cannon stood on top of the fortified platform, which was also equipped with embrasures and occasionally machicolations for launching projectiles onto the enemy. The defensive strategy was quite simple: attackers could be seen in good time, engaged in battle and driven off.

In 1794, the English fought a war on Corsica. The massive tower at Cap Mortella proved a hard nut to crack. For this reason, copies of these so-called *Martello towers* were erected along threatened coasts, Ireland and the Channel Islands included. Eight were built on Jersey, 15 on Guernsey. Their 2.6-m-thick walls taper towards the top, making them appear even more formidable than the 'lightweight' *pre-Martello towers*, as the prototypes came to be called. Twenty-four of the first generation of towers still stand scattered across the islands. The oldest of these occupies a pretty site in the bay *Grève de Lecq.* The best-preserved of the genuine Martello towers is *Kempt Tower.* Other good examples are to be found in *Ancresse Bay* and *Vazon Bay.* Incidentally, none of the Martello towers ever came under attack!

Megalithic monuments

The earliest traces of civilization on the Channel Islands are over 130,000 years old: the so-called megalithic monuments. We

Faldouët Dolmen near Gorey on Jersey, a passage grave dating from 2500 BC

owe the fact that we can still marvel at some of these today to the archaeologist Frederick Corbin Lukis, who led the first excavations in the mid-19th century. In Jersey, 15 out of 60, in Guernsey 10 out of 50 of these historical monuments remain. The others were lost, mainly as a result of ignorance of their true worth, during re-parcelling of land or building work. We distinguish between three generations of dolmen. Firstly, there are the passage graves, in which the burial chamber lies at the end of a long corridor. The oldest grave of this type dates back 5,600 years and is to be found in *La Sergenté* on Jersey. Secondly, the so-called gallery graves comprise several side chambers and are thought to be 4,500 years old. Fine examples can be seen in *La Hougue Bie* on Jersey and *Le Déhus* on Guernsey. Finally, there are the cists, which are built around a common point. They are some 4,000 years old. Standing stones are often found in the vicinity of these burial places, most notably the 3.5-m-high megalith – the tallest surviving example – at *La Longue Roque* on Guernsey. Even today, the Megalithic Period is shrouded in mystery and still throws up more questions than it answers. There is no shortage of theories, but its innermost secrets are safe as yet.

Occupation

To all intents and purposes, it was a peaceful invasion when, on 30 June 1940, German troops landed from the air and sea. They faced no opposition, since the British had pulled out their troops earlier. Initially, both sides endeavoured to keep the consequences of occupation down to a minimum. Life should continue as normally as possible, under the circumstances. Pressure on the islanders was not all too great. Things changed towards the end of 1941, when the Germans began their insane scheme to incorporate the Channel Islands into their Atlantic defences. Thousands of slave labourers were brought in to work almost half a million cubic metres of concrete, suffering inhuman conditions and grave maltreatment. Observation bunkers, anti-tank ramparts, gun emplacements and two underground hospitals were the fruits of these tortuous labours. It was an effort that bore no relation to the strategic value of the islands or to the role they had to play in the conflict: the war was being fought elsewhere. Even 'Operation Overlord', the landing of the Allies in Normandy on 6 June 1944, did not involve the Channel Islands. For one whole year, the islands were cut off from the outside world. Both occupier and occupied endured the same suffering and hunger until they were finally liberated on 16 May 1945.

Smugglers and pirates

Herm and Jethou, its tiny neighbour just a stone's throw away, were ideal hiding places for smugglers and pirates – and there were plenty of them in the 16th and 17th centuries. No passing ship was safe from attack. Should one have managed to escape the clutches of the pirates, there were still the dangerous waters around Herm to contend with. More often than not, the inevitable happened: the ship crashed upon the rocks. Her load and everything that was not nailed down on board fell to the predatory islanders. The idyllic, peaceful islands of today were once dreaded pirates' lairs, to be avoided at all costs. Piracy was not just a feature of Herm and Jethou, but played a role on all the islands. So much so, that, albeit illegally, the foundations were laid for their future prosperity.

Le Seigneur

An absolute novelty in Europe, the feudal-democratic system, introduced over 400 years ago on the small island of Sark by Hélier de Carteret, is still valid today. Like the other Channel Islands, Sark has its own parliament that exercises legislative power, but the Seigneur, the 'Lord of the Island', wields unimpeachable authority. No land may change hands, for example, without the consent of the hereditary island patriarch. If he does give his permission to sell, he receives the so-called *Treizième*, one-thirteenth of the sale price. In addition, the Seigneur is entitled to levy the 'Chimney Tax', also known as *La Poularde*, so called because it was originally paid in chickens! He alone has the right to keep doves and dogs – a privilege anchored in Norman law that was intended to prevent stray dogs killing sheep. In Sark, the Middle Ages are by no means a thing of the past.

Language

Newcomers, getting their first taste of the island towns, could be forgiven for thinking they are in France, looking at the road and shop signs. Again, things are not what they seem. It's true to say that the islanders display many French characteristics, but in their heart of hearts they are British. Logically enough, they speak English, a fact that is taken for granted today, but which was anything but normal in the early Middle Ages. When Duke William conquered England in 1066, he initiated the forced Normanization of the Anglo-Saxons, who were henceforth compelled to assume their new masters' language and way of life. On the Channel Islands, people spoke a Norman *patois*, William's native tongue. As time went by, this dialect was refined and adjusted on each island. These medieval dialects, *Jersiais, Guernsiais, Auregniais* and *Sercquiais*, have survived through the centuries and some islanders still understand and speak *patois* to this day. Cultural societies are trying, albeit with limited success, to preserve these dialects, but it seems inevitable that they will one day disappear.

Pure French, on the other hand, has enjoyed a very different fate. Until 1926, it was the official language of the Channel Islands, but once English got a foothold, there was no stopping its progress. World War II meant the turning point in this linguistic battle. During the German occupation, more than one-third of the islanders fled to England. On their return, after the war, they – and numerous Britons who emigrated to the islands – helped to consolidate once and for all the position of English as the main language. Without a doubt, English is the standard, everyday language, on the street, in the media and administration. French is the language of the law courts, although English is also acceptable. Today, French is seen as an intellectual language, valued for its role in the islands' history and tradition.

Tax haven

Until a little more than 30 years ago, all was right with the world on the Channel Islands. The islanders, fiercely independent and no strangers to hard work, were proud of their healthy agricultural industry and glad of the extra income provided by tourism. On Jersey and Guernsey, there was one savings bank and a handful of branches of English banks. The year 1962 changed all that. The anti-profiteering law, which held interest rates down at a level of 5 per cent, was repealed. The door was opened to dealing in offshore investment funds, such that individuals and companies were able to invest their money

In the spirit of Marco Polo

Marco Polo was the first true world traveller. He travelled with peaceful intentions forging links between the East and the West. His aim was to discover the world, and explore different cultures and environments without changing or disrupting them. He is an excellent role model for the travellers of today and the future. Wherever we travel we should show respect for other peoples and the natural world.

abroad, tax-free. The financial market, a hitherto untapped source of income, rapidly began to flourish. Banks from all over the world began opening branches and placing investments to the value of billions of pounds sterling. These transactions, which poured more and more money into the public purse, prompted a certain unease amongst the islanders. Increasingly, they found themselves open to accusations of having manipulated their tax system in order to attract investors. There was nothing they could do to stop finance outstripping the traditional sectors of agriculture and tourism as the most important economic factor. And so, with every new investment, credit in the islands' treasuries grew, hand in hand with their citizens' secret guilty conscience.

Walking

The best way to discover the charms of the Channel Islands is to walk. Not only is this the best way to experience the well-known spots of natural beauty, but you may even stumble upon some out-of-the-way idyll in the process. On the two smaller islands, Sark and Herm, you often have no choice but to explore on foot. Alderney, too, is a popular destination for keen hikers. Walking tours are offered on Jersey and Guernsey, which take you to the most beautiful areas. One of the best-known walks on Jersey is the *Corbière Walk* (6 km): a 'must' in any hiker's holiday programme. The trail leading from *St Brelade's Bay* to *Beau Port* (2 km) and the path along the beach from *Gorey Village* to *Le Hurel* (3 km) are both outstandingly beautiful. Fascinating, too, is the path along the steep cliffs of the north coast from *Grosnez Point* to *Rozel* (22 km). You don't have to attempt the whole trip all at once, but can divide it up into stages. On Guernsey, the south-east corner in particular sets the hiker's heart racing. The romantic cliff-top path leads from *St Peter Port* on the east coast via *St Martin's Point* along the south coast, taking in magnificent, steep cliffs and coves right along as far as *Corbière Bay* (15 km). The route along the cliffs from *Torteval* around the south-west tip of the island to *Pleinmont Point* (4 km) is also very attractive. What's more, routes are well signposted, so there's no chance of losing your way. Sturdy shoes are a must!

Seafood – out of the net and onto the table

A medley of international ingredients – the recipe for success

Those who are perhaps sceptical about English cooking need not worry. The Channel Islands may be British, but their cuisine is influenced to a large extent by that of their French neighbours. If you had to find a word to describe the contents of the islands' cooking pots, you'd probably choose the adjective 'international', which does not mean, of course, that you won't find any British dishes on the menu. After all, the majority of holidaymakers come from the island on the other side of the English Channel, and they are naturally reluctant to go without their traditional meals when on holiday. Now's your chance to dip into English cooking: you won't be disappointed. Alongside French restaurants, there are also Italian, Portuguese, Greek and Far-Eastern restau-

rants – a real pot pourri of culinary establishments, with the added bonus that it offers something to suit every pocket.

The choice is yours, even at breakfast time: hotels offer English and continental breakfasts, both of which are of a high quality and extremely varied. The classic ingredients are, of course, freshly prepared eggs, teamed up with sausages, bacon and tomatoes. A tasty and satisfying start to your day is guaranteed.

If you prefer a light lunch, you can't go wrong if you choose to eat in a pub. Naturally, the English classics *fish'n'chips* and *pork pies* are on the menu, but you can also try a range of *sandwiches* and other warm dishes to go with your pint. Restaurants and bistros are also open at lunchtime of course. Here you will find sole, perch, plaice and shellfish, caught the same morning and exquisitely prepared. The per-

The Channel Islands boast many good restaurants, like this one in St Helier, Jersey

fect accompaniment to fish are the *Jersey Royals*, delicious, early potatoes and a speciality of the island. In summer, menus also include crab salad, lobster and mussels cooked in white wine. Look out for *le plat du jour*, chalked up on the blackboard. This 'dish of the day' is usually a generous helping of a particular speciality. As is the case in France, it is recommended you choose a set menu, including starter and dessert, as these are often good value for money. To crown it all, you should end your meal with a portion of fresh strawberries and cream. Delicious! Lunchtime is between noon and 2.30 pm.

Fresh cream really comes into its own in the afternoon. Between 3 pm and 5 pm, it's time for the traditional *cream tea*, served in the islands' numerous *tea rooms*. Scones, strawberry jam and a generous portion of clotted cream, washed down with a pot of tea. If the quality of the cream is anything to go by, the cows here must be very happy indeed! For many visitors, *tea time* in the Channel Islands becomes a fixed item on their holiday agenda.

In the evening, the restaurant chefs pull out all the stops. Dinner is not just served, it is celebrated, from start to finish. Appropriately dressed, you take a seat at the bar and enjoy an aperitif while studying the menu. Having placed your order, you can sit back in anticipation of the delights to come. Candlelight enhances the atmosphere at the table. Invariably, the meal lives up to every expectation. Each dish – be it

fresh fish, meat or a vegetable speciality – is of the highest quality, prepared and presented with great skill. Not surprisingly, the islands' cuisine enjoys an excellent reputation. So much so, that even French diners are known to fly over for a weekend, just to savour their neighbours' culinary masterpieces.

A good meal in the evening does not have to cost the earth. From around 6.30 pm, you can go to any restaurant and take a look at the menu, be it a Chinese restaurant, a French bistro or an Italian pizzeria. Pubs, too, offer light meals. Everywhere you go, the islanders' love of eating out in company is apparent. Especially on a Sunday, when the whole family often goes out for a traditional Sunday lunch together. Many restaurants have specialized in catering for this particular group of guests and provide excellent, value-for-money menus. The high point of the culinary year is the 'Good Food Festival', a good-natured contest between the island's chefs, which takes place in May. Holiday guests are especially welcome.

There is no danger that you will die of thirst on the Channel Islands! A wide range of liquid refreshments is available, every bit as good as on the mainland, from wine, cider, beer, spirits to various non-alcoholic beverages. Local products also feature on the wine list. The over 300-year-old *La Mare Vineyards*, for example, owned by the Blayney family, boast a very good Jersey wine. It was this family, too, that created *Grappie*, a mixture of white wine and cider – a partic-

Seafood, fresh and exquisitely prepared: a fish-lover's paradise

ularly refreshing combination in hot weather. The amount of wine produced, however, is too small to warrant marketing on a large scale. The choice of wines on the islands is therefore rounded off with a fine selection of imported French and Italian labels.

On the subject of local produce, we must not forget to mention the milk given by the islands' contented cows! Locals, however, still prefer a beer down at the pub. Whether in the simply furnished *Public Bar* or the slightly more refined atmosphere of the *Lounge Bar*, the draught beers taste equally good, wherever you drink them. Differences are apparent only in the licensing hours, which vary from one island to the next. In Jersey, you can raise your glasses on Mondays to Saturdays from 9 am to 11 pm. The pubs in Guernsey are open on weekdays from 10 am to 11.45 pm. On Sunday, however, alcohol may be served only with a meal, although a light meal or snack is also acceptable in the eyes of the landlord – and the law. Alderney's pubs open daily from 9 am to midnight, with a well-earned break from 2.30 pm to 5 pm in between. Here, in contrast to the other islands, children are allowed to accompany their parents to the pub. They, too, need have no fear of going thirsty!

JERSEY POTTERY

Range
Summer Fruit

Woollen sweaters and fragrant flowers

It's hard to stop at just window-shopping

King Street and Queen Street in St Helier on Jersey and High Street in St Peter on Guernsey are the islands' best-known shopping streets. Here, the shop windows are brimming with all sorts of glittering, shining goods to tempt the passer-by. The Channel Islands are a shopper's paradise, not least owing to the fact that they offer significant tax concessions. Primarily, though, people are drawn here from England and France because retail prices are in many cases some 15 per cent lower than at home. Weekends are an ideal opportunity for a short shopping spree. Other holidaymakers may also find a bargain or simply take home one of the locally produced souvenirs.

If you are a collector, then look no further. Traditionally very popular are the postage stamps from Jersey, Guernsey and Alderney. Banknotes, hot from the press, freshly minted coins and, more recently, telephone cards are much sought-after items.

Arts-and-crafts enthusiasts are bowled over, not just by the heat of the islands' pottery kilns, but also by what comes out of them! Ceramics are high on many visitors' shopping lists. The fact that it is often possible to look over the shoulder of the skilled craftsmen as they work is an added bonus. The art of woodcarvers and coppersmiths can also be admired at first hand. Knitwear is a favourite purchase, mainly on account of its high quality and durability. The famous Guernsey and Jersey sweaters, made of thick, oiled wool, are especially popular. Many of these classic garments find their way into holiday suitcases.

A string of attractive art galleries display works by local artists. Don't forget the antique shops, where you can browse till your heart's content and where you may even find a genuine collector's item.

There are, of course, many natural products that not only look good, but smell delicious too. What better way to capture the atmosphere of the islands, than by taking home some exotic flowers or lavender products? Don't neglect your taste buds either: why not buy some Jersey wine from the La Mare Vineyards to remind you of your holiday?

A favourite amongst souvenir-hunters: island ceramics

27

The 'Battle of Flowers' and much more

The islanders have got celebrating down to a fine art

Any time is the right time for a party, and that's as true here on the Channel Islands as anywhere else. There are plenty of reasons to celebrate throughout the year, and the islands' cosmopolitan population certainly knows how to party.

★ An undisputed highlight on both Jersey and Guernsey is the 'Battle of Flowers', which draws locals and visitors alike out onto the streets. These are exuberant public festivals, culminating in floral processions. If you are holidaying on the islands in August, make a note of the date of the 'Battle of Flowers' in your diary. Such festivals are perfect opportunities to experience local customs at first hand and to meet the people who practise them. It is not possible to list all events here, so do make a point of contacting the tourist information centres upon arrival to find out about forthcoming events. Don't hesitate, just join in! There's no better

The top event on Jersey and Guernsey: the 'Battle of Flowers'

way to make friends and enjoy your holiday to the full.

PUBLIC HOLIDAYS

1 January: *New Year's Day*
Good Friday
Easter Monday
May (first Monday): *May bank holiday*
9 May: *Liberation Day Jersey and Guernsey*
May (last Monday): *Spring bank holiday*
August (last Monday): *Summer bank holiday*
25/26 December: *Christmas*

FESTIVALS & LOCAL EVENTS

January
Alderney: *Battle of the Fireworkers.* New Year's Day

February
Jersey: *Jersey Festival of Cheese.* End of month, one week

March /April
Jersey and Guernsey: *Easter Hockey Festival.* International

29

MARCO POLO SELECTION: FESTIVALS

1 **Battle of Flowers**
Colourful floral
processions in August, on
Jersey and Guernsey
(pages 29 and 30)

2 **Jersey Good Food Festival**
Culinary contest between
island chefs for all to
enjoy (page 30)

3 **Alderney Week**
Mixed programme of fun
and games for young and
old (page 30)

4 **Jersey Irish Festival**
Short celebration of
Irish beer, Irish whiskey
and Irish folk music
(page 30)

hockey tournament. Easter, three days

May

Jersey: *Jersey Air Rally.* International air show. Beginning of month, three days

Alderney: *Milk-a-Punch-Sunday.* Free glass of punch in the island's pubs. First Sunday

★ Jersey: *Jersey Good Food Festival.* Competition between island chefs. End of month, three days

Jersey: *Italian Festival Week.* Mid-month, five days

Jersey: *Portuguese Festival Week.* Second half of month, five days

June

Jersey: *Early Summer Flower Show.* Beginning of month, two days

Guernsey: *International Dance Festival.* Mid-month

★ Jersey: *Jersey Irish Festival Week.* Second half of month, five days

Jersey: *Jersey Festival Rose Show.* End of month, two days

July

Jersey: *St Helier's Day.* Procession. Mid-month

Jersey: *Floral Festival.* Show for garden enthusiasts, with competitions. Second half of month

Sark: *Water Carnival.* Fun competitions held on the water in the harbour. Mid-month

August

Jersey: *Jersey Chinese Week.* Beginning of month, six days

★ Alderney: *Alderney Week.* Varied programme of events. First week

★ Jersey: *Battle of Flowers.* Carnival-style floral festival. Second Thursday

★ Guernsey: *Battle of Flowers.* Carnival-style floral festival. Fourth Thursday

September

Jersey: *International Salon Culinaire.* Competition between master and novice chefs. Mid-month, three days

Guernsey: *Guernsey Festival.* An Arts festival with music, theatre and dance productions. Mid-month, four weeks

Jersey: *International Festival.* Arts festival with opera, jazz, theatre

Jersey Irish Festival Week: not just for those of Irish descent

and dance. End of month, two weeks

The events take place in St Helier on Jersey, in Saumarez Park on Guernsey and in St Anne on Alderney. For further information, consult the information offices.

Summer season

Jersey: *Horse racing at 'Les Landes' track.* From April to August, once or twice per month. In the autumn, numerous agricultural and floral shows are held throughout the islands.

Parade

Once a year, in August, excitement on Jersey and Guernsey reaches fever-pitch. The Battles of Flowers, the biggest festivals in the Channel Islands, fascinate both local residents and visitors alike. Focal point of the event is a giant procession, made up of flower-festooned floats, designed and built with limitless fantasy and great skill. All the other goings-on, ranging from live music to firework displays, contribute to the lively, carnival atmosphere. In the past, the excitement has been so great that some spectators have been known to start the equivalent of a pillow-fight with handfuls of the more than 100,000 blossoms that adorn the floats! Nowadays, these works of art are given safe passage to a museum, where they can be marvelled at by those who missed the festival.

Sandy beaches and steep cliffs

White-crested waves, fine beaches and bizarre cliff formations

Jersey is not only the most southerly and the largest island, it is also the most individual and varied; most fitting superlatives. The island lies 160 km south of England and 22 km from the coast of France. The proximity to her large neighbour makes itself felt in many ways. Despite all outside influences, Jersey is still an endearing world in its own right. The island is approximately 16 km wide and 8 km in length, the terrain sloping gently northwards, from the flat

Jersey boasts superb sandy beaches, such as this one at Portelet Bay

south coast to the northern plateau, which ends abruptly in the bizarre and spectacular cliffs of the north coast.

Basking in the sun and washed by the warm Gulf Stream, Jersey's position means that it enjoys an almost subtropical climate. Consequently, the countryside is varied, boasting lush, green vegetation. Orchid blossoms and camellias provide a splash of colour, set off against exotic palms and eucalyptus trees. The famous *Jersey Royals*, a small, early variety of potato, flourish and the *La Mare Vineyard* produces a delicious wine.

Hotel and restaurant prices

Hotels
Category L: more than £45
Category 1: £30 to £45
Category 2: £15 to £30
Category 3: less than £15

Prices are per person sharing a double room (incl. breakfast).

Restaurants
Category 1: £21 to £30
Category 2: £12 to £21
Category 3: less than £12

Prices are for an aperitif, a main course and a half-bottle of house wine.

MARCO POLO SELECTION: JERSEY

1 St Helier
The highlight of this pretty town is magnificent Elizabeth Castle, lying offshore (page 35)

2 Rozel Bay
This scenic bay, with its picturesque fishing harbour, is quite enchanting (page 44)

3 Noirmont Point
High up on a prominent spot on the south coast, offering a fabulous panorama (page 46)

4 Beauport
Everyone's idea of a quiet, sleepy cove – at least for as long as it stays an insider tip (page 46)

5 La Hougue Bie
Neolithic place of worship, the oldest surviving structure on the Channel Islands, with a long passage grave and a burial chamber (page 40)

6 Plémont Bay
Framed by steep cliffs, at low tide, this has to be the most beautiful beach on the island (page 51)

7 Mont Orgueil Castle
Historic fortress overlooking the row of romantic houses in the port (page 42)

8 Les Mielles
Once a refuse dump, today a stunningly beautiful nature reserve with over 400 species of flowers (page 51)

9 St Brelade's Bay
Elegant resort on the exotic south coast, with a touch of the Côte d'Azur (page 47)

10 St Aubin
Enchanting harbour with fort lying offshore, at the western end of beautiful St Aubin's Bay (page 45)

It's only a small step from 'sunny island' to 'holiday paradise'. Jersey's natural features are such that the holidaymaker's expectations are well catered for. One of the main attractions is the sun-drenched south coast, with its cosmopolitan, lively capital, chic resorts and cosy sandy bays. Sports enthusiasts are drawn to the long west and east coasts. For those who prefer a little peace and quiet, the cliff-top paths along the deeply fissured northern coastline, with its secluded coves, are ideal. Nature-lovers are in their element in the centre of the island. Here, it seems all is still right with the world and the countryside is uniquely beautiful.

It is important to remember that the island is small, a mere 116 sq km. It would be easy to cover the main features of the island quickly by car. However, you will find that, scarcely have you entered what appears to be a major settlement on the map, you have left it again. It is much more enjoyable to walk, cycle or ride along the *Green Lanes* from one part of the island to another. This is surely the best way to do justice to a landscape that is hard to beat.

ST HELIER

☛ **City Map inside back cover**

(108-109/C-D4-5) To judge by its population statistics, St Helier, with its 35,000 inhabitants, is a small town. Nevertheless, it vehemently stakes its claim to the title of undisputed centre of the island. And rightly so, for it is without a doubt a busy and exciting town.

This was not always the case. The foundation by monks, in 1155, of St Helier's Priory marked the beginning of centuries of calm. Later, Elizabeth Castle was built on the foundations of the priory. The small, tranquil market town was transformed into a busy port, as St Helier became the starting point not only for cod fishing expeditions to Newfoundland, but also a base for piracy. Affluence grew steadily as time went by. The turning point came in 1846, when Queen Victoria of England officially opened the *Victoria Pier*, and with it the gateway to the world. In return, the world came to visit the sunny islands in the English Channel and laid the foundations of the flourishing tourism industry. This alone, however, was not sufficient to secure the prosperity of the island. Tourism is responsible for less than one-fifth of the credit side of the island budget. A good 60 per cent comes from the booming financial sector. The Channel Islands are a tax haven, financially independent offshore centres, offering favourable conditions for financial, banking and insurance deals. There is no value added tax, capital gains tax or gift tax, no death duties are levied and no taxes are deducted at source. The influx of vast amounts of money from the English and European mainland shows no signs of diminishing. Consequently, the islanders have got their hands full, managing funds, trusts, industrial insurance and, above all, private assets. And they are true masters of their craft. The islands are doing very well thank you! So much so, that it is sometimes difficult to find suitable investment opportunities for the profits resulting from these financial transactions. One such investment, however, was the construction of an extensive harbour area, able to operate independent of tidal movements, which otherwise have a detrimental effect on waterways. Such developments are symptomatic of the desire to leave the past behind and prepare for the future. Everywhere, the thirst for modernity is evident. Fortunately, the essential characteristics of this endearing town remain untouched by these new trends. Let's hope it stays that way.

SIGHTS

Elizabeth Castle   (U/A4)
★ On a prominent site, picturesque Elizabeth Castle flanks the harbour entrance in St

Commanding and impregnable: Elizabeth Castle off St Helier

Aubin's Bay. At low tide, the mighty fortress can be reached on foot across a 750-m-long causeway. Amphibious vehicles, lovingly nicknamed *ducks*, connect the island and the mainland at high tide. In the evening, when the castle is floodlit, the scene is particularly stunning, an impression that is confirmed when you take a tour around the island. In the space of four centuries, mighty fortifications have been built up around the immense central tower. It takes approximately two hours to look around the entire site. We recommend you time your visit to coincide with the traditional gun salute ceremony at midday. *End of Mar–Oct; daily 10 am–5 pm; admission: £3.50.* Lying just off the coast on a rocky islet is the 11th-century *St Helier's Hermitage*, named after the patron saint of the town.

Fort Regent (U/B4-5)

Towering over the town on a ridge stands a large leisure centre, which brings in countless visitors with its various attractions. Changes to the complex are currently under consideration, the aim being to find an exterior that blends in more effectively with the town's appearance. The unconventional

Corbière Walk

Just before the turn of the 19th century, there really was a railway line on Jersey. It ran originally from St Helier to St Aubin and was later lengthened to cover the six kilometres to Corbière. The trains and the tracks are a thing of the past, but what remains is the embankment, along which runs the Corbière Walk. The footpath is a pleasant walk, and there are benches at the viewpoints, inviting you to rest for a while. You can cover the route in one and a half hours. Cyclists are, of course, faster but present no hazard to hikers. The path takes you past countless spots of natural beauty and ends at breathtaking *La Corbière* with its brilliant white lighthouse upon wild cliffs. All you need to do is get going and discover Jersey at its finest!

nature of the site and, above all, ☙ the marvellous view over the town and St Aubin's Bay make it well worth visiting. *Daily 9 am–9 pm; admission depending on activity*

King Street (U/B4)
In the most popular shopping street on the Channel Islands, you will find a seemingly endless string of shops and boutiques. The neighbouring streets and lanes, too, boast tempting displays. Once you get started, it's difficult to stop bargain-hunting, especially since the prices are usually just as tempting as the products themselves.

Market Halls (U/C4)
A gem amongst Victorian iron architecture is the *Central Market* on *Halkett Place*. At the entrance, prettily framed by the cast-iron embellishments, is the Jersey coat of arms. In the middle of the hall stands a bubbling fountain, surrounded by the many stands with their displays of the many fruits of the island's agricultural industry.

A few steps further on is *Beresford Market*, where the spirited voices of the traders can be heard praising their selections of fresh fish and various types of seafood. *Mon–Sat 9 am–5 pm; Thurs until 12.30 pm*

Royal Square (U/C3)
A secluded spot in the middle of town. If you're tired of window-shopping, you can rest on a shady bench below the chestnut trees or at the bar of a pub. For centuries, *Royal Square* was the market place. Today, the gleam-

Royal Square: Statue of George II

ing gold *statue of George II* is surrounded by the prestigious buildings that house the *Royal Court*, the former *Public Library* and the *States Chambers*, home of the island parliament. The reddish façade of the 14th-century *Town Church* can be glimpsed in the background.

MUSEUMS

Jersey Maritime Museum (U/B5)
The museum documents the strong link between the island and the sea. On your tour of the museum, you can test your skills in the wave canal and experience the power of the sea's currents. The influence of wind and weather on the islands is also demonstrated, together with the many ways in which man exploits the sea for his own purposes. The *Occupation Tapestry Gallery* is housed in a former storehouse. Local women have hand-woven 12 tapestries to commemorate the fiftieth anni-

St Helier is a shopper's paradise, especially the Market Halls

versary of the liberation of the island. *North Quay; daily 10 am–5 pm; admission: £3.80*

Jersey Museum (U/B4)

An impressive account of the history of the island is given in an old 18th-century warehouse on *Liberation Square*. The focal point of the exhibition is the Victorian era. A 12-minute video presentation at the start of the tour is a helpful introduction for the visitor. The *Barreau Le Maistre Art Gallery* on the upper floor contains a collection of works by Jersey artists past and present. *The*

Weighbridge; Mon–Sat 10 am–5 pm; admission: £3.20

RESTAURANTS

Albert J. Ramsbottom (U/C4)

Highly original restaurant – not to be missed! *Fish'n'chips* and other English classics are on the menu. Large portions and good value for money as well. *90 to 92, Halkett Place; Tel. 72 13 95; category 3*

Belgo (U/B4)

The house of 101 Belgian beers. Monastic setting, right down to the waiters dressed in monks' habits. *10, Wharf Street; Tel. 72 91 00; category 2*

Candlelight Grill (U/A4)
German head chef presents international cuisine in stylish, candlelit setting. *Kensington Place; Tel. 61 11 11; category 2*

Longueville Manor Hotel (109/D5)
The most elegant place to eat out in Jersey. Award-winning, top-class restaurant in a magnificent 13th-century manor house, set in a handsome park in the heart of the island. *Longueville Road (A 3); Tel. 72 55 01; e-mail: longman@itl.net; category 1*

Museum Brasserie (U/B4)
Good international and British cooking, served in pleasant surroundings, adjacent to the museum. *The Weighbridge (Jersey Museum); Tel. 51 00 69; category 2*

Nelson's Eye Restaurant (U/C6)
Here you will find a range of mouth-watering fish dishes and fresh seafood. The pretty view out over the sea is included in the price! *Havre de Pas; Tel. 87 51 76; category 2*

SHOPPING

Don't just stand outside, with your nose pressed up against the window! Go on in, and get shopping! The displays of the many jewellers' shops in King Street and Queen Street are filled with a tempting selection of all that glitters.

High-quality items are also to be found at camera dealers, hi-fi shops and perfumeries. Although no value added tax is levied in the Channel Islands, the strength of the British pound could dampen your eagerness to spend.

If you want to get an impression of the island's shopping culture, then *De Gruchy*, *King Street* and *New Street* are the places to go. The largest department store in the Channel Islands stocks an interesting selection of goods. As St Helier is a veritable shopper's paradise, it is difficult to resist the temptations on offer – even if you really want to. Rummaging amongst the stalls of the *Open Air Market* is an enjoyable way to pass the time. Here, you'll find reasonably priced antiques and jewellery, textiles and, of course, souvenirs. *Hope Street; Apr–Oct; Sat 8.30 am–4.30 pm*

ACCOMMODATION

Hotel Christina (U/A3)
Lying above wide St Aubin's Bay, this pleasant, middle-class hotel boasts a fantastic view over the bay and Elizabeth Castle. *62 rooms; St Aubin's Bay; Tel. 75 80 24; Fax 75 80 24; category 1*

Grand Hotel (U/A3)
Luxurious hotel, standing directly on the promenade. Not only is the accommodation excellent, *Victoria's Restaurant* offers top-quality menus. *115 rooms; Esplanade; Tel. 72 23 01; Fax 73 78 15; category L*

Hôtel de France (U/C4)
Large, elegant house on the outskirts of town, with indoor swimming pool, whirlpool and sauna. The hotel's own *Gallery Restaurant* offers gourmet meals

in the evenings. *320 rooms; St Saviour's Road; Tel. 61 40 00; Fax 61 41 99; category 1*

Longueville Manor Hotel (109/D5)

This tastefully renovated manor house is regarded as the best hotel in the Channel Islands. Magnificent park. Its quiet, out-of-town setting makes this a place of refuge where you can let yourself be pampered. *32 rooms; Longueville Road (A 3); Tel. 72 55 01; Fax 73 16 13; e-mail: longman@itl.net; category L*

Hotel Revere (U/A3)

Competently run, pleasant hotel, close to the centre of town. *58 rooms; Kensington Place; Tel. 61 11 16; Fax 61 11 16; category 1*

SPORTS & LEISURE

❂ The indoor leisure centre at *Fort Regent* is the ideal venue for sports and games, whatever the weather. Swimming, gymnastics, badminton, squash, table tennis, billiards and lots more. *Daily 9 am–9 pm*

ENTERTAINMENT

The islanders like a good time and visitors are more than welcome to join in. The range of entertainment on offer is large; there's something to suit all tastes, all year round.

Theatre, nightclubs, discos and cabaret: the standard is good, occasionally very good *(for up-to-date information, consult Jersey Tourism).*

The fun starts at *Fort Regent* in the afternoon, a varied pro-gramme, alternating between revues, shows to concerts. Posters give details of what is currently on the bill. *Jersey Tourism* also offers information.

❂ Dance till you drop at *Raffles Night Club, Halls, 13, James Street.* The *Jersey Arts Centre* in *Phillips Street* is a combined theatre and art gallery, staging concerts, dance, mime and other events.

A real treat in the evenings is a tour of the town's many, highly original pubs. *The Peirson* on *Royal Square* is a fine example. Jazz fans can swing to good live music at *The Blue Note at 20, Broad Street.*

INFORMATION

Jersey Tourism

Liberation Square; May–June, Mon–Sat 8.30 am–7 pm, July–Sept, 8.30 am–8 pm, Oct–Apr, 9 am–6 pm; Tel. 50 07 77; Fax 50 08 08

SURROUNDING AREA

La Hougue Bie (109/E4)

★ The 5,500-year-old Neolithic burial site is the oldest surviving structure in the Channel Islands. Under a massive earth mound, a 22-m-long passage grave leads to a chamber, which served as a heathen place of worship in the prehistoric era. Seventy upright stones support 16 capstones. A curator of the site offers guided tours on Wednesday afternoons. On top of the dolmens stand the 12th-century *Notre Dame de la Clarté Chapel* and the adjoining 16th-century *Jerusalem Chapel*, which can also be visited.

The history of civilization on two levels: La Hougue Bie below two chapels

The museum of the *Société Jersiaise* is nearby *(Apr–Oct, daily 10 am–5 pm; admission: £2.90)*, and shows not only archaeological finds, but illustrates the geology and early history of the island. During the Occupation, the Germans established their headquarters on this site. As a reminder, the *German Occupation Museum* stands here today. At the junction of the B 28 and B 46. *End of Mar-Oct, daily 10 am-7 pm; admission: £3.50.* 2 km

Samarès Manor   (109/D5-6)

A very fine example of the island's typical Norman manor houses can be found on the estate of the former Seigneur of Jersey. The manor dates from the 19th century and is still lived in today. The nearby dovecote is part of the original Norman structure, built in the 12th century, and is consequently the oldest of its type on Jersey. The guided tour of the manor house gives an insight into the lifestyle of earlier residents.

In the park, the herb garden, with its 150 types of herb, is well worth seeing. Here, 15 almost forgotten varieties of thyme are lovingly nurtured; many of these were used in the past as flavourings and for medicinal purposes. The restaurant in the grounds serves particularly tasty herb and vegetarian dishes. *Inner Road, St Clement; Apr–Oct, daily 10 am–5 pm; guided tours: Mon–Sat mornings only; admission: £3.50.* 4 km

THE EAST

The route around the eastern half of the island leads along the coast road to the beach at *Grève d'Azette* and to *St Clement's Bay*, culminating in *La Rocque Point*. ⤷ At low tide, seen from the headland called *Green Island*, which separates both bays, a broad landscape of bizarre cliffs and reefs is revealed. It's not until you reach the *Royal Bay of Grouville* on the east coast of the island that you find a sizeable expanse of beach. At *Gorey*, the land begins to slope up towards the steep cliffs of the north coast.

A typical image of Jersey shows the chain of 16 *Martello Towers* that stand along the east coast. They were built at the end of the 18th century to guard against French attack. Today, they are privately owned.

GOREY

(109/F4) The main attraction on the east coast is this small port, which lies below the massive fortress *Mont Orgueil Castle*. The breathtaking view, straight out of the guide books, is just begging to be photographed. What appears today to be merely a good subject for a photo, was once a nightmare for the French. During the Hundred Years' War, they tried on numerous occasions, though without success, to capture this powerful stronghold. For centuries, the port was an important centre for trade and the fishing industry. When the once-profitable trade in oysters moved elsewhere, things rapidly quiet-

ened down in Gorey. It was the influx of holidaymakers that breathed new life into the town, and tourism is the most important source of income today.

SIGHTS

Faldouët Dolmen (109/F4)
Interesting Neolithic graves close to the church in Gorey recall the early history of the island. The 15-m-long passage grave is thought to be 4,500 years old. The huge capstone probably weighs around 24 tonnes. *Free admission*

Mont Orgueil Castle (109/F4)
★ It is possible to reach the fortress by car, though it is much more interesting if you approach it via the flight of steps from the harbour.

⤷ With each step climbed, the magnificent panorama across the town, harbour and bay becomes more and more breathtaking. The closer you get to the structure, the more you can appreciate its sheer size. Starting in the lower courtyard, you ascend through various levels to reach the central courtyard, the heart of the castle. Next to the simple *St Mary's Crypt*, an exhibition in the keep illustrates, by means of reconstructed scenes and an audio-visual display, the history of the 13th-century castle. *Daily 9.30 am–6 pm; admission: £3.50*

RESTAURANT

Jersey Pottery Restaurant (109/F4)
Set in the flower-filled gardens of the pottery is a popular restaurant, whose exquisitely prepared and diverse range of fish

dishes has earned it a reputation as a Mecca for the island's lovers of fine food. The *plateau de fruits de mer* – the seafood platter – is highly recommended. *Rue de la Potterie; Tel. 85 11 19; Mon–Sat noon–3 pm; category 1*

SHOPPING

Jersey Pottery   (109/F4)
Visitors can not only look around the workshops and see the production of the island's typical ceramics, but can also shop here for pretty and reasonably priced souvenirs. *Rue de la Potterie; Mon–Sat 9 am–5.30 pm*

ACCOMMODATION

Beausite Hotel   (109/F4)
Overlooking the Royal Jersey Golf Course, the hotel is situated somewhat outside Gorey itself. Pool, sauna and fitness room. *76 rooms; Grouville Bay; Tel. 85 75 77; Fax 85 72 11; category 2*

Old Court House   (109/F4)
Just a few minutes' walk from the harbour, on the edge of town. Quiet, pleasant building with swimming pool, sauna and solarium. *57 rooms; Gorey Village; Tel. 85 44 44; Fax 85 35 87; category 1*

SURROUNDING AREA

Anne Port   (109/F4)
Just along the coast from Gorey, the cliff *Jeffrey's Leap* marks the beginning of the rocky coastline, which climbs towards the north. Popular destinations for bathers – both locals and visitors – are *Petit Portelet Bay*, *Havre de Fer* and, above all, *Anne Port.* 1 km

Bonne Nuit Bay   (108/C1)
The islanders have a saying: whoever sails around *Le Cheval Guillaume*, the rock that stands in the middle of the bay, on Midsummer's Eve, shall have good luck in the coming year. A visit to this picturesque cove with its fine, sandy beach at low tide is a stroke of luck in itself. 9 km

Bouley Bay   (109/D-E2)
Many years ago, the caves in the tall, granite cliffs surrounding this beautiful, sandy bay were the hiding places of smugglers and pirates. To deter the local inhabitants from interfering with their dubious activities, they invented a story about a huge, black dog with gleaming red eyes, which was said to roam around below the cliffs. The Black Dog Pub in the Water's Edge Hotel harks back to the gruesome tale.

The Durrell Wildlife Conservation Trust   (109/D3)
This quite remarkable mini-zoo is a collection of animals, brought together in 1959 by writer Gerald Durrell with great care and compassion.

The park, measuring only 3 sq km, is home to several interesting species, whereby the gorillas are easily the most popular attraction with visitors. The objective of the subsequently founded *Jersey Wildlife Preservation Trust* is the breeding and re-establishment in the wild of endangered species. The highly successful research centre has acquired a solid reputation worldwide. The cost of the research carried out here is high,

Gorillas are a main attraction at the Durrell Wildlife Conservation Trust

harbour, which attracts many bathers at low tide, on account of its sheltered position, despite having only a pebble beach.

An absolute gem amongst the houses of the village is the much-photographed *Apple Cottage* (picture on page 7), with its fabulous front garden. 4 km

Hotels/restaurants: *Château La Chaire Hotel.* Quiet, pleasant atmosphere. The exquisite restaurant is decorated in the Edwardian style. *14 rooms; Rozel Bay; Tel. 86 33 54; Fax 86 51 37; category 1. Le Couperon de Rozel.* Neatly incorporated into a Napoleonic fort on the beach. The restaurant serves fresh and value-for-money fish dishes. *35 rooms; Rozel Bay; Tel. 86 55 22; Fax 86 53 32; category 2. Apple Cottage Restaurant.* You can not only dine well here, but should also come along in the afternoon, at tea time. *Rozel Bay; Tel. 86 10 02; daily 11.30 am–10.30 pm; category 2*

though the price of the entrance tickets is a small, but vital contribution to meeting it. A visit here is therefore recommended on all counts. *La Rue ès Picots (B 31), Trinity; daily 9.30 am–6 pm; Nov–Apr, till dusk; admission: £6.* 6 km

Royal Bay of Grouville (109/F5)

Grouville, with its long, sandy beach, numbers several Martello towers amongst its attractions, which were built during the Napoleonic Wars. The Seymour Tower and Icho Tower can both be reached on foot at low tide. 2 km

Rozel Bay (109/E2)

★ Your holiday agenda should definitely include a visit to this small fishing village. Beautifully situated on the lush green slopes of the bay, this is without doubt one of the loveliest spots on the island. Focal point is the idyllic

St Catherine's Bay (109/F3)

Directly adjacent to the Havre de Fer and the *Archirondel Tower,* a striking, red-and-white Martello tower marks the start of St Catherine's Bay. It stretches as far as *Verclut Point.*

In Victorian times, plans were drawn up to build a naval port in the bay. All that remains of this ambitious project is *St Catherine's Breakwater* – an 800-m-long mole, the ideal place for a walk out into the sea. The shingle beach attracts many bathers to the bay, despite the lack of sand. 2 km

THE WEST

The broad semicircle that is beautiful St Aubin's Bay leads to the varied westerly stretch of the south coast. Elegant resorts, tranquil coves and precipitous cliffs are set in lush green vegetation and a multitude of colourful flowers: a fascinating and, above all, lively corner of the island.

The dominant image of the flat, west coast is one of seemingly never-ending sandy beaches. These are populated chiefly by water-sports enthusiasts, braving stiff winds and rolling waves on their surfboards.

Nestling amongst the dunes behind the coast road is the nature reserve *Les Mielles*. Early summer sees the famous Jersey orchid coming into flower, one of around 400 different species of plant that grow here.

At the northern end of this section of coast, the landscape is transformed once more into one of steep cliffs and curious rock formations framing sandy coves.

ST AUBIN

(108/A5) ★ This charming little port sits snugly in the hills at the western end of St Aubin's Bay. Impressive houses and cobbled streets exude peace and tranquillity.

Quite a different picture presents itself in the harbour area, characterized by romantic, narrow lanes. If you come by car, you'll have trouble finding a parking space, especially if you intend to make this the starting point of your hike along the famous *Corbière Walk* to the southwest tip of the island.

SIGHTS

Harbour (108/A5)
Main attraction of this small town is its sizeable harbour with its numerous yachts and boats. A stroll along the quay wall might prompt you to take a break at one of the string of local restaurants and pubs, which are busy, but worth a visit.

St Aubin's Fort (108/A5)
Standing on a rocky islet off the coast is the peaceful-looking fort, ⋙ from which you have a good view of the harbour, the town and the hills round about. The fort is accessible on foot at low tide.

Shell Garden (108/A5)
West of St Aubin, a winding road takes you up onto the plain. As you leave the town, you can see an enchanting little house, whose walls are covered from top to bottom in seashells.

MUSEUM

Hamptonne Country Life Museum
It is still possible to find many farmhouses on Jersey built in the typical Norman style: solid stonework, prominent chimneys and a wall around the farmyard and garden to protect against the persistent winds.

The museum is housed on the estate of the Hamptonne family, the buildings having been completely renovated inside and out to reflect their original state.

In the main house, which dates from the 17th century, visitors can learn about the way farmers lived in previous centuries. An exhibition illustrates the history of agriculture on Jersey, with the aid of historical photographs and documents.

The fruit trees in the pretty orchard have also been laid out in the old style, and the apple orchard has its own fully functional copy of an original cider press. *Rue de la Patente; Apr–Nov, daily 10 am–5 pm; admission: £3.50*

RESTAURANT

Old Court House Inn

Historic house that attracts a lot of visitors. Don't be put off by the crowds, though; it's worth a try, just for the atmosphere. Fish specialities and seafood mouth-wateringly prepared – you won't leave the table feeling hungry. *Harbour promenade; Tel. 74 64 33; category 1*

SHOPPING

Jersey Lavender Farm (107/F4)
The smell of lavender is in the air as you enter St Brelade. The 55 varieties cultivated here delight with their fragrance, especially in May and June, when the plants are in flower. Farm products can be purchased in the shop. *St Brelade, Rue du Pont Marquet; May–Sept, Mon–Sat 10 am–5 pm; admission: £2*

ACCOMMODATION

Somerville Hotel

Situated above the harbour. Pool, bar with sea view. *59 rooms; St Aubin; Tel. 741 22 96; Fax*

74 66 21; sommerville@jerseyhol.com; category 1

The Panorama

Pleasant, privately owned guest house, with a pretty tea garden and a wonderful sea view. *17 rooms; La Rue du Croquet; Tel. 74 24 29; Fax 74 59 40; www. jerseyisland.com/staubin/panorama; category 2*

SURROUNDING AREA

Beau Port (107/E5)
★ Insiders will tell you that this is the most beautiful place to bathe on the island. Quiet, sandy cove lapped by the turquoise-blue sea, close to *St Brelade's Bay*. The climb down the cliff – and up again – is hard work though! 4 km

La Corbière (107/E5)
A most dramatic picture presents itself to the visitor on the south-west tip of the island: precipitous cliffs and an angry sea hurling spray and foam at the coast. In the midst of all this stands a brilliant white lighthouse, just waiting to be photographed. It can be reached on foot at low tide. ⚐ From here, you get a splendid view of the entire west coast. 9 km

Noirmont Point (108/A6)
★ Set on a high cliff, where gorse and heather intermingle with concrete bunkers, is a most spectacular viewpoint. The ⚐ panorama of the whole south coast and the sea is breathtaking. It's a shame that the site was ruined during the war by the erection of a command centre. 3 km

Portelet (108/A6)

Along the quay in this pretty little fishing harbour stands a row of cottages belonging to ship's captains and lighthouse keepers. Close by is the *Table des Pions*, a round, grass-topped mound, surrounded by a stone circle. The site is steeped in legend relating to the Michaelmas ride, a heathen ceremony originating in the Middle Ages.

Portelet Bay (108/A6)

At the foot of the Noirmont cliffs, accessible only via a flight of steps, is this charming, sandy bay, popular amongst bathers, who value its secluded position. Lying opposite, just off the coast, is the tiny *Ile au Guerdain* with its Martello tower *Janvrin's Tomb*. 3 km

Restaurant: *Old Portelet Inn*. Seventeenth-century guest house, high above the bay, serving small, good-value dishes. *Portelet Bay; Tel. 74 18 99; category 1*

St Brelade's Bay (107/F5)

★ ✿ When it comes to bathing attractions, this semicircular bay is a real gem. Fringed with palm trees and exotic flowers, the sandy beach offers you ample space for all kinds of beach activities and water sports. Directly adjacent are several top-class hotels. For those who prefer a little peace and quiet, *Ouaisne Bay*, the eastern part of the beach, is the ideal choice. Worth seeing in the village itself is *St Brelade's Church*, which is said to date from the sixth century. *The Fisherman's Chapel* with its beautiful 14th- and 15th-century frescoes should also not be missed. 3 km

Hotels/restaurants: *Golden Sands Hotel*. High-class hotel with direct access to the beach. *62 rooms; St Brelade's Bay; Tel. 74 12 41; Fax 49 93 66; category 1*. *L'Horizon*. Best hotel on the beach with elegant restaurant *Star Grill*. *107 rooms; St Brelade's Bay; Tel. 74 31 01; Fax 74 62 69; category L*

ST PETER'S VILLAGE

(107/F3-108/A3-4) Idyllic is the best way to describe the heart of the island, where mother nature has really done herself proud! The bright, cheerful valleys, in particular, stir the imagination: *Vallée des Vaux, Waterworks Valley, Bellozane Valley*. The most beautiful must surely be *St Peter's Valley*, with its lush, green meadows, fields and woods. A walk along here sets every nature-lover's heart beating faster. *St Peter's Village* is important on account of its proximity to the airport.

Visible for miles around is the 37-m-high tower of *St Peter's Church*. Otherwise, the village is unspectacular, preferring to blend quietly and harmoniously into the surrounding countryside, as do all the other villages on the island.

SIGHTS

German Underground Hospital (108/B4)

Oppressive reminder of a tragic period is this huge underground hospital, hewn from the rock by slave labourers during the German Occupation of the island in World War II. Two kilometres of long, damp tunnels lead to rooms that served partly as hospital facilities, partly as ammunition stores. *Meadowbank, St Lawrence; daily 9.30 am–3 pm; admission: £4.80.* 2 km

Jersey Flower Centre (108/B2)

Those who like carnations will be amazed at the sight of the greenhouses at the centre. With an annual crop of over six million blooms, this is the largest cultivator of carnations in the United Kingdom. Irrigation alone swallows up more than 200,000 litres of water per day. The paths between the greenhouses total almost 20 km in length.

You can watch the staff cutting, sorting and packing the carnations and treat yourself to a beautiful bouquet to take with you.

In the gardens in front of the greenhouses, flamingos stalk about, while geese and ducks swim on the pond. In the midst of all this, you'll find a miniature town, on a scale of 1:12. *Retreat Farm, St Lawrence; daily 9.30 am–5 pm.* 3 km

Living Legend Park (108/A3)

It calls itself 'Jersey's No. 1 Attraction', and it certainly is extra special. The main feature is a 22-minute multimedia show, illustrating the history of the island with the aid of numerous special audio and visual effects.

A restaurant, a children's playground and a souvenir shop round off the choice of activities – all in all, quite an experience for the whole family. *Rue de Petit Aleval, St Peter; Apr–Oct; daily 9.30 am–5.30 pm;*

Mar/Nov, Sat–Wed 10 am–5 pm; admission: £5.10. 1 km

Moulin de Quetivel (108/A4)

Nestling in a picturesque bend of St Peter's Valley lies the Moulin de Quetivel, one of eight mills that once operated on the river. It was built in 1309 and its wheel turned for over 600 years, until the invention of the steam engine brought an end to its working life. Informative displays give an insight into the history of the island's mills and the work of the miller. *Mont Fallu; May–Oct, Tues–Thurs 10 am–4 pm; admission: £1.50.* 2 km

MUSEUMS

Battle of Flowers Museum (107/E2)

More than 100,000 flowers go to make up the fantastic decorations on each float that takes part in the annual floral procession on the second Thursday in August. Those who miss the event on the day can marvel at these veritable works of art in the museum. *La Robeline, Mont des Corvées; mid-March–mid-Oct, daily 10 am–5 pm; admission: £2.50*

Jersey Motor Museum (107/F3)

❖ A colourful and impressive mixture of old military vehicles, fire engines and luxury cars. The owner enjoys talking shop with vintage- and veteran-car fans, eagerly showing off his finest exhibit, the Rolls Royce Phantom III, which belonged to the British General Montgomery. *St Peter; Apr–Oct, daily 10 am–5 pm; admission: £2.50*

Paradise for outdoors and sports freaks

If you're looking for a sporting kick, Jersey offers you some interesting new opportunities. The wild, deeply fissured cliffs in the north of the island are the ideal setting. What about rock climbing, high above the raging sea, on the granite cliffs close to ruined Grosnez Castle? Coastal traversing is a combination of swimming and climbing along the cliffs at low tide. If you want to set your adrenaline level soaring, then go for abseiling, letting yourself down the cliff face at Noirmont or the rocks at St Catherine by rope – great fun! The least extreme of the new popular sports is canoeing. If you want to find out more about these activities, please contact Mick Cullinane at Rock & Roll Adventure Sports, La Rue des Bessieres, St Lawrence; Tel. 0044/1534/86 38 35

RESTAURANT

Greenhill Country Restaurant (107/F3)
A pleasant atmosphere accompanies the international dishes on the menu, topped off by a well-stocked wine cellar. *Coin Varin; Tel. 48 10 42; category 2*

The Star & Tipsy
Toad Brewery   (107/F3)
Brewery with its own in-house pub, serving a range of snacks. Very cosy and inviting. *St Peter's Village; Tel. 48 55 56; category 3*

SHOPPING

Jersey Pearls   (108/B2)
If you like pearl jewellery, you've come to the right place: beautiful rings, earrings and other items, some of them made here in the workshop, which means they aren't necessarily expensive. *St John's Village; Mon–Sat, 10 am–5.30 pm*

La Mare Vineyards   (108/A2)
The mild climate permits the cultivation of wine on the island. The wine pressed here at the seat of the Blayney family from Jersey grapes has only one shortcoming: there isn't enough of it! If you want to try it, you can taste the wine at the shop. Here, you can also buy home-made jams and mustard as souvenirs. *St Mary; Apr–Sept, Mon–Sat 10 am–5.30 pm; admission: £3.75*

Micro World   (109/D2)
Art en miniature. The works of Spaniard Manuel Ussa can be admired only through a magnifying glass. Some even require the assistance of a microscope, such as the figures of Adam and Eve, carved out of the tip of a pencil. *Five Mile Road; Apr–Oct, daily 10 am–5.30 pm*

ACCOMMODATION

Greenhill Country Hotel   (107/F3)
Pleasant atmosphere following renovation work. *25 rooms; Coin Varin; Tel. 48 10 42; Fax 48 53 22; category 1*

SURROUNDING AREA

Devil's Hole   (108/A1)
The climb down to the bay *Les Reuses* – and afterwards back

Already over 600 years old: Moulin de Lecq

up again – is rather steep and difficult, but it's worth the effort: at the end of the path, you can take a look into the 'Devil's Hole': a gaping hole, gouged out of the rock by the sea, through which jets of spray threaten to drench curious spectators at high tide. ❧ While you're there, don't forget to admire the fascinating cliffs.

Restaurant: *Priory Inn* Back up on 'dry land', this pub gives you a welcome opportunity to get your breath back. *Category 3.* 5.5 km

Grève de Lecq (107/F1)

Popular amongst bathers, this bay is one of the most beautiful spots on the north coast, framed as it is by high cliffs and blessed with a fine, sandy beach at low tide. For many years, this landing place was heavily guarded. The oldest Martello tower, built to ward off French attack, still stands, looking rather out of place in the middle of a car park. The *Grève de Lecq Barracks* used to house a garrison of British troops. The *Barracks Visitor Centre* includes exhibitions describing the history and the natural history of the north coast. 3 km. Restaurant: *Moulin de Lecq.* A cosy and inviting restaurant, popular with day-trippers. Reasonably priced meals are served indoors and in the garden of this 600-year-old mill, whose wheel still turns today. *On the B 40; category 3*

Grosnez Point (107/D1)

The navigational light that warns mariners of the dreaded *Paternoster Rocks* stands amidst the foam-tipped breakers as they thunder onto the shore. Above it, on top of the granite cliff, stand the remains of *Grosnez Castle*, which was destroyed in the Hundred Years' War. From here, you can see not only along the wild and rugged coastline, but you may get a glimpse of the other Channel Islands, too. Romantics and keen photographers take note: ⚜ this spot is famous for its amazing sunsets. 6 km

Les Mielles (107/E3)

★ The Mielles dunes behind the wide beach at *St Ouen's Bay* were neglected for many years and consequently were in a desolate condition. It was not until 1980, when the authorities stepped in and cleared away the accumulated debris that nature was free to reclaim what was once hers. Between the leisure area in the north and a golf course to the south, a nature reserve of unparalleled beauty has been created. The grassy hills, dense vegetation and a lake skirted by reed beds constitute an ideal habitat for numerous species of flora and fauna. Islanders and visitors alike delight at the rare plants and animals that have re-discovered the area and settled down here. Observation paths and ornithological tours *(May–Sept, Thurs 3 pm)* reveal and explain the natural wonders of Les Mielles. *Kempt Tower* on the coast road houses *Les Mielles Visitors' Centre (May–Sept, Tues–Sun 2 pm–5 pm, Oct–Apr, Thurs, Sun 2 pm–5 pm)*, which presents a graphic illustration of flora and fauna of the dune area – at no charge. 1.5 km

Plémont Bay (107/D-E1)

★ At low tide, this sleepy little cove, nestling between the cliffs, is one of the prettiest on the island. When the tide comes in, however, the fine, sandy beach disappears. Pop into the beach café to make up for the disappointment. 6 km

St Ouen's Bay (107/D-E2-4)

The broad, sandy beach extends over almost the entire length of the west coast. To prevent enemy landings, a quay wall was constructed during World War II, which now rather abruptly separates the beach from the dunes, and ★ the unique nature reserve *Les Mielles*. Without a doubt, the wall has its uses: it prevents the huge waves from eroding the shoreline, thus causing irreparable damage to the beautiful west coast.

❀ The bay also is the venue for *sand racing.* Offshore, wind and waves afford ideal conditions for surfing. Some 800 m off the southerly part of the coast, the striking *La Rocca Tower,* yet another Martello tower, stands clear of the water. It can be reached on foot at low tide. 2 km

Bathing coves and cliff-top paths

Crystal-clear water, sun-drenched beaches, breathtaking cliffs

There is probably no satisfactory way to settle the bone of contention that divides the island rivals: which island is more beautiful? Both share many similarities, but display sufficient unique characteristics to allow their inhabitants to be especially proud of 'their' island. Visitors who experience the islands in a holiday mood are prepared to accept each island for what it is, and Guernsey certainly has a lot to offer.

With a total area of 64 sq km, Guernsey is only half the size of her sister island Jersey. The decision to give its capital, St Peter Port, a central position on the island was a wise one, bringing many benefits. The town is ideally situated, providing access to all the resources of its hinterland. For this reason, many people who work in St Peter Port, for instance, can afford to live in the countryside or on the coast and travel the short distance each day to work. This is just one example, and there are many more.

The cliff-top path along the south coast of Guernsey is famous, and rightly so

The backbone of the island's prosperity is the finance industry. As on all the other islands, taxes here are very low and exert an almost magical attraction for investors from all over the world. Against this background, the island administration can quite safely invest in the improvement and expansion of the tourism industry, the second most important branch of the island's economy. The high expectations that holidaymakers bring with them are satisfied to a very large extent.

The natural beauty of the island plays a vital role here. Dazzling white beaches on the north coast contrast starkly with the imposing cliff landscape of the south. In between lie idyllic valleys with lush, green vegetation, blessed by the mild climate. To be able to enjoy all this on a walk along the cliffs or on a cycle tour is surely a very special holiday experience.

Although greenhouses still seem to dominate the landscape, the agriculture industry is no longer of such importance as it was in earlier years. Flower cultivation and milk production are now at the forefront of the countryside industries. For many years now one of the most successful export articles has been the much-praised tomato, the *Guernsey Tom*, as it is lovingly called. Its high quality makes it very popular amongst consumers in Great Britain and on the continent.

Naturally enough, visitors will also find this delicacy on the menu, exquisitely prepared in the island's excellent kitchens. In addition, lobster, crab and other seafood, fresh from the waters around the island find their way onto the table. Fish-lovers certainly can't go wrong when they come to Guernsey. Specialities from all over the world feature on the island's menus, too, and, what's more, they come in all price classes and are always mouth-wateringly prepared and served.

If you are driving round the island on a Sunday, looking for a good restaurant perhaps, then make sure your petrol tank is full – Sundays really are a day of rest here, as far as the retailers are concerned. The church doors are wide open, but elsewhere, in pubs and discos, for example, you'll find them closed. The filling stations sell all sorts of things on a Sunday – except petrol.

ST PETER PORT

☛ **City Map inside back cover**

(105/D-E3-4) ★ Those of you who approach St Peter Port by ship will

---

MARCO POLO SELECTION: GUERNSEY

1 St Peter Port
This really is the most beautiful town in the Channel Islands and deserves the No. 1 spot (page 54)

2 Castle Cornet
Magnificent fortress, built to protect the capital (page 55)

3 Moulin Huet Bay
Not easy to get to, but all the more enjoyable when you do (page 68)

4 Little Chapel
A piece of religious art, which fascinates also non-believing spectators (page 66)

5 La Grandmère du Chimquière
Historic standing stone, with charming legend to boot (page 66)

6 Ste Apolline's Chapel
The little chapel with the big heart – a true historical gem on the island (page 62)

7 Sausmarez Manor
Seat of the family to whom the island owes so much (page 66)

8 Fort Grey
Fortress with a difference in a bay with a difference (page 61)

9 Beaucette Marina
Where the island's millionaires keep their yachts (page 64)

10 Maison Victor Hugo
Last, but not least: memories of a famous guest from France (page 57)

surely not forget your first glimpse of the capital: the mighty fortress lying offshore, a veritable sea of masts in the harbour and the splendid houses and graceful towers of the town itself, which seem to clamber row by row up the steep slopes beyond. All these elements together make up a classic picture-postcard image. The long promenade, wrenched from the sea, links the impressive harbour area with the pretty town. Prestigious houses in the Regency and Victorian styles and the steep, cobbled streets, narrow lanes and flights of steps all combine to give the visitor the impression he is standing on a film set. The quiet charm of what after all is a mini metropolis overlays the busy goings-on of the locals and the hustle and bustle of the tourists in the shopping streets framed by historic houses. All in all, an enjoyable sense of leisureliness pervades the town, making it all the more attractive.

If you were to turn back the pages of the history books to the 11th century, you would discover that St Peter Port is one of the oldest communities in the Channel Islands. The *Town Church* is mentioned as early as 1048. The strategically favourable position of the town forms the basis for its importance for seafarers through the centuries. In order to underline this fact, the construction was begun back in 1204 of *Castle Cornet*. The transition from what was still a small fishing port to the busy town we know today began taking place at the end of the 18th century, when piracy was legalized by the British Government, leading to the expansion of the settlement and an increase in prosperity.

Around 1800, St Peter Port had become a town of affluent businessmen and merchants. As a consequence of this, the modest houses dating from the Middle Ages had to make way for more stylish, prestigious buildings. The influx of new residents during the Napoleonic Wars meant that the town expanded, taking in the slopes behind it and the plateau above. At first, the harbour was unable to keep up with these developments. It was not until the mid-19th century, that the area was re-built and indeed extended to reflect its true standing. Today, St Peter Port is home to some 19,500 inhabitants, who are all convinced that they live in the most beautiful town in the Channel Islands. Countless visitors willingly share this opinion.

SIGHTS

Castle Cornet (U/F3-4)

★ The magnificent fortress, which was built at the beginning of the 13th century to protect against French invaders, stands off the coast, opposite the harbour: a most picturesque sight. Nevertheless, the French succeeded on two occasions, a century later, in capturing the fortress. However, they managed to hold on to it for only a short time. The fortress tower fell victim to a fire when it was struck by lightning in the 17th century. The appearance of the fortress today is largely the result of the renovation work and new additions made after the fire. Previously, the fortress was inaccessible at high tide; now, however, an 800-m-long mole links it to the mainland. In the main guard room, you can find out more about this sprawling stronghold. This first exhibition prompts you to seek out the other four museums housed in the fortress, which illustrate the turbulent and moving history of the island. A special feature of the castle that cannot be overheard is the traditional military ceremony and gun salute. *Apr–Oct, daily at noon. Fortress: daily 10 am–5 pm; admission: £2.50 (free admission for children)*

French Halles (U/E3)

On the Market Place, you will find the large, over 100-year-old market halls – as always, a hive of noisy activity. This is especially true of the fish hall, where, in the mornings, stall-holders extol the virtues of their freshly caught fish and delicious seafood, their voices ringing loud and clear across the floor. Watch as the lobster, crayfish and prawns are tossed into bubbling pots to be cooked and then soon afterwards packed, still piping hot, into customers' shopping bags. Things are just as hectic in the other halls, where the island's agricultural produce is on display. This is a good opportunity to try a bag of those famous tomatoes or strawberries, which are too good to miss!

High Street (U/E3)

The busiest shopping street on the island is High Street, which leads into *Le Pollet*. Behind the stylish façades of the historic town houses, influential financiers have their offices upstairs, above the attractive shops and businesses on the groundfloor. It's quite possible to find a bargain in the *Viaer Quatre*, which extends as far as *Trinity Square*. This romantic part of the old town is characterized by densely packed rows of shops,

boutiques and antique dealers and begins at the lower end of High Street. Those who wish to demonstrate their sporting prowess should climb the 111 *Arcade Steps* – in one go, of course. The reward for such exertion is a splendid view of the harbour and fortress, seen across the town roofs below: well worth the effort.

Royal Court House (U/E3)

This impressive building, which dates from the 18th century, is the seat of the island parliament. Visitors are permitted to observe sessions from the public gallery and thereby gain an insight into the workings of island democracy. *Rue de Manoir*

Town Church (U/E3)

From the 11th century onwards the church, which stands on the quay of the *Albert Pier*, has dominated the townscape. It is a massive, granite structure, which has been altered on several occasions over the centuries. Each individual building phase and its architectural style can be discerned. For example, remains of the arch from the 12th-century Norman St Helier Chapel can still be seen in the chancel.

The interior is particularly interesting on account of the impressive bishop's throne and carved wooden pews.

Guernsey Museum (U/E2)

If, during a walk around town, you should make your way up to *Candie Gardens*, in their elevated position above St Peter Port, then have a short break at the tea pavilion and savour the view over the town, harbour and bay. You could even visit the *Guernsey Museum and Art Gallery* and discover a wealth of information on the eventful history of the island and its fascinating archaeological legacy. *Daily 10 am–5 pm; admission: £2.50 (free admission for children)*

Maison Victor Hugo (U/E4)

★ ⟨⟩ High above the town, with a breathtaking view of the harbour and fortress, stands the extravagant town house in which the French writer spent some 18 years of his exile. It was here that he penned some of his finest works. Everything has been carefully preserved, just as Victor Hugo left it when he returned to Paris in 1870. The heirs presented the house to the city of Paris as a gift, so that, transformed into a museum, it could serve as a fitting tribute to its famous inhabitant. *Hauteville House, 46 Hauteville; Apr–Sept, daily 10 am–noon and 2 pm–4.45 pm; admission: £3*

The Four Seasons (U/E3)

The specialities of the house are its fine fish dishes and wonderful puddings. *South Esplanade; Tel. 72 74 44; category 2*

La Frégate (U/E2)

This is a gourmet restaurant, especially when fish or seafood is being served. Included in the price is the fine view over the town and the harbour. *Les Cotils; Tel. 72 46 24; category 1*

Nino's (U/E3)

Pleasant restaurant serving Italian specialities and, of course, an excellent Chianti. *Lefebvre Street; Tel. 72 30 52; category 2*

Victor Hugo (105/E4)

If you like lobster, this is the right address for you. The restaurant, belonging to the St Pierre Park Hotel specializes in this and other excellent seafood dishes. *Rohais; Tel. 72 82 82; category 1*

St Peter Port: first impressions are seldom wrong

Victoria Pier   (U/E3)

A ideal place to conclude your tour of the town and harbour, relaxing over a good meal. *Victoria Pier; Tel. 70 00 61; category 3*

Shopping excursions are also amongst the highlights on the Guernsey tourist's agenda. Although the British pound is currently very strong, the lack of value added tax goes some way to redressing the balance. Probably not far enough, though, so do shop around and compare prices. Items produced locally are amongst the most popular purchases, such as the silver jewellery made by Bruce Russell.

❧ Don't forget to visit the picturesque *weekly market*, which is held every *Thursday from 1 pm to 5 pm* in summer on the Market Place. The islanders, many dressed in traditional costume, make a good subject for a photograph, as they show their displays of island produce. Look out for the stall selling masses of delicious vanilla ice cream – it's a real hit!

In *Cornet Street*, you will find the oldest and best-preserved town house in St Peter Port. Today it is home to a reconstruction of a typical Victorian general store, the *National Trust Shop*, and is well worth a visit. In it, you can buy all sorts of odds and ends and souvenirs.

Those of you with a sweet tooth should try *Rebecca's Pralines*, delicious chocolates made from *Guernsey cream milk* to Rebecca Davis's recipes. And if you don't mind itchy wool next to your skin, you'll find the world-famous Guernsey sweaters in the shops for around £25–£30.

Popular amongst collectors are the Guernsey postage stamps, which can be obtained at the *Philatelic Bureau* in *Smith Street*. A 'must' for all toy fans is a visit to the *Toy Factory*, which produces, amongst other things, the Guernsey Teddy, a celebrity not only on the island and a lovely souvenir for children.

Duke of Normandie   (U/E4)

In a quiet position, but just one minute away from the High Street, this comfortable hotel in the style of an 18th-century *maritime inn* has its own restaurant and bar. *37 rooms; Lefebvre Street; Tel. 72 14 31; Fax 71 17 63; category 2*

Hotel de Havelet   (U/E3)

This quietly situated, elegant hotel has the air of a noble gentlemen's club and is appropriately accommodated in a period Georgian house. Standing high above the harbour, it offers a panoramic view of Castle Cornet and the surrounding area. *34 rooms; Havelet; Tel. 72 21 99; Fax 71 40 57; category 1*

Old Government House   (U/E3)

Rich in tradition, the hotel stands halfway up the hill overlooking the harbour and the sea. Tasteful and elegant throughout with a good restaurant. *72 rooms; Ann's Place; Tel. 72 49 21; Fax 72 44 29; category 1*

Somerset Hotel   (U/D3)

A friendly, family hotel on the outskirts of town. The rooms are well appointed and the cooking is just like at home. *36 rooms; Queen's Road; Tel. 72 27 25; Fax 71 36 12; category 3*

As if time has stood still: a farmhouse on Guernsey

The St Pierre Park   (105/E4)

The best hotel on the island. Secluded location in its own park on the outskirts of town. Here you are offered the finest standards of comfort and cuisine. A nine-hole golf course, tennis courts and indoor swimming pool complete the picture. *130 rooms; Rohais; Tel. 72 82 82; Fax 71 20 41; category L*

SPORTS & LEISURE

The waters around the islands are very popular amongst the sailing fraternity; one look at the sea of yachts' masts in the *marinas* at St Peter Port confirms this. Lovers of all other types of sport, such as tennis, golf, horse-riding and, not to forget, water sports are guaranteed their fair share of fun on Guernsey.

◉ In St Peter Port, the *Beau Séjour Leisure Centre* is not only a 'Mecca' for theatre and concert enthusiasts, but offers a wide range of sporting facilities for keen sportsmen and -women, be they young or old, including squash, badminton, table tennis and swimming.

ENTERTAINMENT

An ideal way to spend an evening is to pay a visit to one of the local *pubs*. You could easily combine this with a stroll through the town's cobbled streets. ⟰ If you prefer the disco atmosphere, you'll find just the right thing at *Les Folies d'Amour* in *North Plantation* and at *Club 54* in *Le Pollet*. Entertainment shows, theatre productions and concerts are staged regularly at the *Beau Séjour Leisure Centre* – watch out for advance notices!

INFORMATION

Guernsey Tourist Board   (U/E3)

North Plantation, St Peter Port; Mon–Fri 9 am–5 pm, Sat 9 am–4 pm,

Sun 9.30 am–12.30 pm; Tel. 72 35 52;
Fax 71 49 51

Château de Marais (105/E3)
Here, on the edge of town – not exactly one of the nicer places to live – you'll find, if you look hard enough, the remains of a medieval castle, surrounded by a moat. Built in the 13th century, the complex was renovated during the Napoleonic Wars. The remnants that can be seen today of what is also known as *Ivy Castle* date from this period. 4.5 km

Fort George (105/E4)
Guernsey is not only visited by countless tourists, but also many affluent foreigners who would like to settle down here. In an effort to control this influx, the property market has been segmented. The number of houses available on the *open market* is limited to 2,000. Islanders can acquire property only on the *local market*, at much more realistic and reasonable prices. Numerous millionaires' estates are located south of town in *Fort George*, above *Soldiers Bay*. 1 km

THE NORTH

The 40-km round-trip of the island can easily be accomplished by car in one day. The island's most beautiful spots, however, deserve to be experienced at a more leisurely pace. One possibility would be to follow a route along the lovely beaches of the northern half of the island. Alternatively, take the route along the cliffs of the impressive, steep coastline of the southern half.

COBO

(104/C3) The western end of the first route suggested above touches on three parishes. *Castel* is noted for its beautiful sunsets, *St Saviour* has the largest number of art treasures on the island and, finally, *St Peter in the Wood*, which boasts the largest bay. The parishes border on one another, linked together by the impressive coast road. But don't be tempted to neglect the charming countryside of the hinterland. Cobo, situated on the most beautiful bay, is an ideal starting point for tours of the westerly section of the northern half of the island.

Câstel (105/D3)
Excavations carried out under the church of *St Mary of Castel* brought to light a *standing stone* dating from prehistoric times. Today, it stands in front of the entrance to the *parish church*. The stone was presumably worshipped as a type of 'mother-deity'. The interior of the church is decorated with beautiful 14th-century frescoes.

Cobo Bay (104/C3)
Those who consider themselves experts on Guernsey are unanimous in their opinion: this is the best place to watch the sun go down.
⚜ One thing is for certain, the steep climb up to *Fort Guet* is rewarded with a superb view across the bay (and of the sunset). Cobo Bay and the adjoining *Vazon Bay* boast inviting, sandy beaches that attract countless swimmers and sunbathers. Both bays are also ideal for surfing and windsurfing.

MUSEUMS

Fort Grey Maritime
Museum   (104/A5)

★ The fort's white tower houses a maritime museum with very varied exhibitions. The immensely dangerous seas off the western tip of the island have caused many ship to sink or run aground here over the centuries. The museum documents not only these accidents, but also records the history of navigation, and shows underwater archaeological finds made in the area. *Rocquaine Bay; daily 10.30 am–5 pm; admission: £2.* 14 km

Guernsey Folk Museum   (105/D3)

Saumarez Park, the largest park on the island, is the home of the Guernsey Folk Museum, a group of reconstructed farmhouses that graphically illustrate life on the island in days gone by.

Historical costumes, fully furnished reconstructions of living quarters and antiquated agricultural tools have been lovingly collected and put on display. *Saumarez Park; Apr–Oct, daily 10 am–5.30 pm; admission: £2.50.* 5 km

SHOPPING

Oatslands Craft Centre   (105/E2)

Here at the craft centre is a large selection of skilfully made copper and brass articles, which are also for sale. How about taking back an original Guernsey milk can as a reminder of your holiday? *Braye Road, Vale; daily 9.30 am–5.30 pm.* 4 km

ACCOMMODATION

Cobo Bay Hotel   (104/C3)

Situated directly on the coast road, this expertly run hotel is ideally placed for watching the beautiful sunsets for which Cobo is famous. It also has its own excellent restaurant. *36 rooms; Cobo, Castel; Tel. 571 02; Fax 545 42; category 2*

La Grande Mare Hotel   (104/C3)

Top-class hotel on Vazon Bay with an 18-hole golf course, a swimming pool and a private lake for angling. The *Golf and Country Club* also includes a superb restaurant and well-stocked wine cellar to delight its guests. *27 rooms; Castel, Vazon Bay; Tel. 565 76; Fax 565 32; category L*

L'Atlantique Hotel   (104/B4)

Small and quiet, this hotel stands in its own park overlooking Perelle Bay. The restaurant is noted for its mouth-watering, fresh seafood dishes. *23 rooms; Perelle Bay, St Saviour; Tel. 640 56; Fax 638 00; category 2*

SURROUNDING AREA

Le Friquet Butterfly
& Flower Centre   (105/D3)

Le Friquet is a tranquil spot. You can almost hear the wing-beats of the many exotic and indigenous butterfly species in the *centre's* hothouse. Here, surrounded by subtropical plants, a habitat has been created for the insects, which seems to suit them very well.

Visitors can observe the cultivation of native flowers in the greenhouses and, after that, select an appropriate souvenir from the shop. *Le Friquet; Apr–Oct, daily 10 am–5 pm; admission: £2.* 3 km

Lihou Island/L'Erée   (104/A4)

The rocky islet lies off the northwest tip of the island, and can be reached via an old causeway at low tide. Apart from the remains of a medieval monastery, dating from the 12th century and once owned by the monks of Mont St Michel, the tiny island has little to offer the visitor.

A look around on *L'Erée* peninsula is a more promising activity. Here, you'll find prehistoric dolmens. The unique *Le Creux ès Faies* is located right on the tip of the island. Thought to be some 4,000 years old, it measures 9 m in length and is therefore the third-largest passage grave in Guernsey.

Erected approximately 1,000 years earlier is the *Trépied Dolmen*, which lies at the southern end of nearby Perelle Bay. Several stone uprights and capstones of this 6-m-long passage grave survive.

L'Erée is overshadowed by a tower constructed during World War II. At its foot is a pleasant café. From here, you can see across to *Fort Saumarez*, which is privately owned and consequently not accessible to the public. 12 km

Pleinmont   (104/A5)
Barren and overgrown with heather, the Pleinmont peninsula juts far out into the sea from the south-west corner of Guernsey. It is covered with a network of footpaths affording breathtaking views out to sea.

Standing on the coastal path, which runs between here and *Fermain Bay*, you can see across to *Hanois Rock*, which, until the construction of the lighthouse in 1862, was the cause of numerous shipwrecks.

If you turn your attention away from the sea for a moment, you might discover along the way the ruin of the *haunted house* that Victor Hugo described in his novel *Les Travailleurs de la Mer*, and which served as an observation point for customs officials when keeping a look-out for smugglers and pirates.

Pezeries Point   (104/A5)
This is probably the loneliest spot on the Channel Islands – it certainly lies furthest to the west. The mighty fortress is a relic of Napoleonic times.

Rocquaine Bay   (104/A4-5)
This most impressive bay stretches for almost 3 km between *Pezeries Point* and *Lihou Island*. At low tide, a bizarre landscape is revealed: daunting, jagged cliffs enclosing pretty, sandy coves. This is not only a lovely place to swim, but also offers ideal wave conditions for surfers. In the southerly part of the bay, on a flat expanse of rock, stands *Fort Grey*, one of the island's three Martello towers. It was built in 1804 to protect the island against invasion and presents quite a striking picture to the onlooker. The main body of the structure is of grey granite, the tower in the centre is painted white, an image that gives rise to its nickname amongst the locals of 'cup and saucer'. Today it houses the *Maritime Museum* and is accessible via a causeway. 14 km

Ste Apolline's Chapel   (104/B4)
★ Measuring just 9 m in length and 4 m in width, this pretty 14th-century chapel is one of the island's architectural treasures. It is dedicated to the patron saint of dentists. During restoration of the chapel, the frescoes on the interior walls were refurbished. The image of

Historic furnaces at the Oatlands Craft Centre in St Sampson

the Last Supper, also dating from the 14th century, is particularly beautiful. *Mont Saint, La Grande Rue; daily 9 am–8 pm.* 11 km

ST SAMPSON

(105/F2) In the north-eastern part of the island lie densely populated St Sampson and *Vale*, surrounded on three sides by the sea. These are two of the ten parishes that constitute the administrative districts of Guernsey. To reach them, you must take the route along the rocky *Belle Grève Bay*. The harbour at St Sampson is characterized by its cranes, shipyards, warehouses and oil tanks – evidence of the hard work that is done here. It is here that cargo vessels landing at

Guernsey are unloaded, and a large proportion of the incoming goods are processed in the vicinity. There is, consequently, not much room for touristic highlights. The town is nothing to write home about, but it serves as a good base for excursions to the eastern part of the picturesque north coast, such as the trip across the site of the *Braye du Valle*, a tidal channel between St Sampson and *Grand Havre*. Until 1806, this effectively cut off Vale from the remainder of Guernsey. A bridge was the only link between the 'mainland' and this offshore island. The salt marshes here are now a legally protected area. For reasons of military security, the channel was filled in and, as a result, 300 hectares of land was reclaimed from the sea. As so often in Guernsey, greenhouses dominate the scene today.

St Sampson Church   (105/F2)
You might find it hard to drag yourself away from the shops and cosy harbour pub on the main shopping street *The Bridge*, but we recommend you make the effort to visit the village church, just a short distance away. This simple, welcoming Norman building dates from the 12th century and is well worth a second look. The tower and saddle roof make a pretty subject for a photograph. Inside one of the two chapels are niches containing old tombstones that hark back to before the Reformation. *Church Street*

RESTAURANT

Blind O'Reilleys   (105/F3)
Typical Irish pub serving traditional stews and fish dishes. Cosy and lively atmosphere. *South Side; Tel. 24 45 03; category 3*

SHOPPING

Guernsey Candles   (105/E2-3)
Visitors can watch as the candles are being made and decorated with great skill. Naturally, these works of art can be purchased as souvenirs. *St Sampson, Les Petites Capelles; daily 10 am–5 pm*

Oatlands Craft Centre   (105/F2)
Two furnaces betray the previous function of the site: the craft centre occupies a former tile factory. The potters are more than willing to let visitors watch them at work and are naturally very pleased if their skilfully crafted designs find an interested buyer. Their products make popular holiday souvenirs. *St Sampson, Braye Road; daily 9.30 am–5 pm*

ACCOMMODATION

L'Ancresse Bay Hotel   (105/E-F1)
The hotel stands between the lovely beach in the bay on one side and one of the island's golf courses on the other. It has a good restaurant and an indoor swimming pool. *24 rooms; L'Ancresse Bay, Vale; Tel. 24 43 28; Fax 24 34 93; category 2*

Peninsula Hotel   (105/F2)
Enjoy your holiday right next to the beach with a view across Grand Havre Bay. This very well-appointed hotel also boasts fine cuisine, a swimming pool and children's playground. *99 rooms; Les Dicqs, Vale; Tel. 24 84 00; Fax 24 87 06; category 1*

SURROUNDING AREA

Beaucette Marina   (105/F1)
★ As you approach the harbour, the first thing you see are the tips of white sails against the grey cliffs of the coast. It is only when you reach the quay wall that you realize the marina is man-made, on the site of a former quarry. The harbour entrance was hewn out of the rock to open up a pretty anchorage for ocean-going yachts.

L'Ancresse Bay   (105/E-F1)
The sandy beach here is over 2 km long and therefore very popular with families. The little ones can build sandcastles, the older children and adults can surf to their heart's content. Six of the twelve watchtowers, built in 1778

to protect the island, still stand guard over the beach, their upper platforms once armed with mighty cannons. 5 km

Le Déhus Dolmen   (105/F2)

The second-largest passage grave on the·island is thought to be over 3,000 years old and is covered by an earth mound.

On entering, it's 'lights on and heads down' for the 10 m until you reach the main chamber. The illumination of the roof reveals the outline of a human figure, armed with bow and arrow. Not surprisingly, he has been named *Le Gardien du Tombeau*, guardian of the grave. *Paradis; daily from 9 am; free admission.* 1 km

Les Fouaillages   (105/E2)

On *L'Ancresse Common*, which gently encloses the bay of the same name, you will find one of the island's golf courses. At the fifth hole, close to *Ladies Bay*, the burial chambers known as *Les Fouaillages* lie hidden. They have only recently been discovered, and have been partly reconstructed. The burial site dates from about 4000 BC, and is of interest not only to archaeologists.

Just a stone's throw away to the north, the largest megalithic passage grave in Guernsey was discovered in 1811. *La Varde Dolmen* measures some 12 m in length and is covered by six huge capstones. *Off L'Ancresse Road.* 5 km

La Rousse Tower   (105/E2)

The Channel Islanders lived for centuries in fear of French invasion, the people of Guernsey being no exception. Here, the flat, north coast was regarded as being particularly vulnerable to enemy attack.

During the Napoleonic era, a long chain of mighty, round forts was constructed along the coasts to protect the island. The restored La Rousse Tower is a fine example of the architecture of these watchtowers, with its cannon and embrasures, and gives an insight into the life of the garrison stationed there. Ironically, the towers were never seriously under threat of attack.

Vale Castle   (105/F2)

A fort is believed to have stood on this site as early as the Iron Age. The remains that can be seen today are part of a structure built in the 17th century.

The outline of the site gives an indication of the huge dimensions of the castle in its heyday. It is possible to walk along the perimeter wall, where a fine panoramic view can be had. *Castle Road; free admission*

THE SOUTH

The route cuts right across the island from the lush, green vegetation of the east coast, along the cliffs of the south coast up to the barren plateaus of the west.

This is an enchanting route, which gives the visitor the chance to see the parish of *St Andrew* in the heart of the island, and also the parishes of *St Martin, Forest* and *Torteval* in the south, with their breathtaking cliffs and romantic coves.

ST MARTIN

(105/D-E5) The road from St Peter Port to the parish of St Martin leads through secluded valleys and dense woodland. Driving across the countryside to the precipitous coastline, with its cliff-top paths

The seat of one of the most influential families on Guernsey: Sausmarez Manor

and idyllic bays, it's easy to understand people's enthusiasm for Guernsey. A point of reference on this route is the village of *St Martin*, which is situated approximately 3 km from the capital.

SIGHTS

La Grandmère du Chimquière (105/E5)
★ The so-called 'Grandmother of the Cemetery' is one of the most-photographed monuments on the island. The granite standing stone, which stands at the entrance to the churchyard at St Martin, dates from about 2500 BC. The visible crevice in the 160-cm-high statue is said to have been made by a clergyman, enraged at the respect the figure commanded amongst parishioners. *St Martin, parish church*

Little Chapel (105/D5)
★ Famous far beyond the bounds of the island is this, the smallest Catholic church, measuring only 5 m in length. This imitation of a grotto in the church at Lourdes was painstakingly constructed over a period of many years by the French monk Déodat. Tens of thousands of fragments of pottery, glass and sea shells have been pieced together to form a giant mosaic, covering inside and outside walls. For some, the result is a tasteless 'pile of rubbish', though most people find it fascinating and consider it a masterpiece, a most delicate and complicated jigsaw puzzle. Little Chapel was able to take up its intended function only at the third attempt, because the bishop who was to consecrate it was unable to enter through the doorway, on account of his generous proportions! *Les Vauxbelets.* 6 km

Sausmarez Manor (105/E5)
★ The name *Sausmarez* is heard often on Guernsey. The family, which can trace its ancestors back to the year 1254, is one of the most distinguished dynasties on the island. By rights, candidates for the

office of *Bailiff* and *Governor* have often been drawn from their ranks.

The family seat, a manor house dating back to the 13th century, is one of the finest buildings on the island, noted for its 18th-century Queen Anne façade. Visitors taking a tour of the house are particularly impressed by its valuable and antique furnishings; the large park, too, is magnificent, having a sizeable stock of very old trees. A pleasant and relaxing way of touring the park is by means of a mini railway.

If it could talk, the house would certainly have some interesting stories to tell. Even the fabled treasure of the Incas would get a mention. In the first half of the 18th century, soon after losing the family property, Philip de Saumarez took command of the *Centurio*. His aim, as part of a small fleet, was to make life hard for the Spaniards in America. Just off the Philippines, he boarded a Spanish galleon, which was carrying so much Inca gold, that it subsequently took 32 carts to transport it to a vault in London. Incidentally, Philip's ship was the only one to return. His happiness was short-lived, however, since he died in a sea battle not long after he had succeeded in buying back the family property. *St Martin, Fort Road, Manor House; Easter–Oct, Mon–Thurs 10 am–noon, June–Aug 10 am–noon and 2 pm–6 pm; admission: £4.50*

MUSEUMS

German Occupation Museum   (104/C5)
The museum consists of a comprehensive display of interesting documents from the time of the German Occupation, alongside impressions of life on Guernsey during the war years. *Route de Petit Bôt; Apr–Oct, daily 10 am–5 pm; admission: £2.50.* 3 km

German Underground Hospital   (105/D5)
During a period of over three years, more than 60,000 tonnes of rock had to be hewn out of the ground to complete this project. Many of the slave labourers did not survive this torturous experience. Finally, the occupying Germans used the site for nine months as a field hospital. The 2,000 m of tunnels have since been emptied and left very much as they then looked. It seems unlikely that visitors, confronted with this sinister backdrop, will ever fully comprehend this act of madness. *La Vassalerie Road; daily 10 am–noon and 2 pm–4.30 pm; admission: £2.50.* 2 km

RESTAURANT

La Barberie   (105/E5)
Highly recommended is the three-course menu, not only because it tastes delicious, but also because the price is right. *Saint's Bay, St Martin; Tel. 23 52 17; category 2*

SHOPPING

Guernsey Clockmakers   (105/D5)
Time becomes a work of art in the hands of the master clockmaker in his workshop, situated close to Little Chapel. His clocks and barometers function just like any conventional model, but they are infinitely more attractive. Maybe you would like one of these timepieces as a reminder of your holiday? *Les Vauxbelets;*

Mon–Fri 8.30 am–5.30 pm, Sat 10 am–4 pm. 6 km

Moulin Huet Pottery (105/E5)

The pottery, which is situated in a pretty valley close to *Moulin Huet Bay*, is not easy to find, but luckily there are some helpful signposts. Here, typical Guernsey pottery is produced and sold at reasonable prices. *Moulin Huet Bay; Mon–Sat 9 am–5 pm, Sun 10 am–12.30 pm.* 3 km

ACCOMMODATION

Bella Luce (105/E5)

This small, granite manor house is located close to picturesque Moulin Huet Bay. Red roses on the outside and a charming atmosphere inside, with its spotless and comfortable rooms. The restaurant prides itself on its fine menus and the pub serves good meals. *33 rooms; La Fosse, St Martin; Tel. 23 87 64; Fax 23 95 61; category 2*

Green Acres Hotel (105/E5)

A quiet, rural setting for this elegant, very well-appointed hotel. Excellent cuisine and its own swimming pool. *48 rooms; St Martin, Les Hubits; Tel. 23 57 11; Fax 23 59 78; category 1*

La Michelle (105/E5)

This small, cosy hotel stands out in the countryside, just a few minutes from *Fermain Bay*. Heated swimming pool. *14 rooms; St Martin, Les Hubits; Tel. 23 80 65; Fax 23 94 92; category 3*

La Trelade Hotel (105/E5)

This hotel, housed in a traditional Guernsey country house, ensures a pleasant and comfortable stay. Heated swimming pool. Chil-

dren welcome. *45 rooms; St Martin, Forest Road; Tel. 23 54 54; Fax 23 78 55; category 1*

SURROUNDING AREA

Fermain Bay (105/E5)

This charming bay with its beautiful, sandy beaches is a popular destination, especially with families. The gently sloping beach enables even very small children to splash and play safely at the water's edge. The path up to the romantic coastal footpath is guarded by a most imposing Martello tower. From here, this well-known footpath takes you along the attractive south coast to *Pleinmont Point.* Nearby stands the *Doyle Column*, which was erected in honour of Governor Sir John Doyle, who was in office during the Napoleonic Wars.

⬩⬩ The renovated monument deserves a visit, especially since it brings with it a superb panoramic view over the coast, the islands and the sea.

Fermain Bay can be reached by boat from St Peter Port. 2 km

Moulin Huet Bay (105/E6)

★ This corner of the island in the south-east must surely be the most beautiful section of coastline on the island. Moulin Huet Bay, with its delightful coves *Petit Port* and *Saint's Bay*, is highly recommended for a day trip. They lie directly below the high cliffs, which form countless tiny niches and secluded corners. These can be reached only on foot, which means there's plenty of room for those who do make the effort to get there. French artist Auguste Renoir, who came here from Paris in 1883, was fond of painting the bathers here in this picturesque setting. 3 km

At low tide, one of the loveliest bays on Guernsey: Moulin Huet Bay

Jerbourg Point (105/F6)

Jerbourg peninsula forms the south-east tip of Guernsey. The landscape is both beautiful to look at and of great historical significance. Excavations have shown that it was inhabited as early as the Neolithic Age. Graves and earthworks were constructed here in the Bronze Age, and a castle that stood here in the Middle Ages served as a sanctuary for the islanders at a time when the French held Castle Cornet.

Petit Bôt Bay (105/D6)

As the name suggests, this is one of the smallest, but also one of the most beautiful bays for bathing in. Opening out at the end of a delightful valley, the bay presents itself in true romantic vein, rounded off by its Martello tower and former water mill, which today houses a café. The fine, sandy beach lives up to every seaside holiday expectation. 3.5 km

The island with a difference

An island for the aspiring – and the accomplished – individualist

In Alderney, things are slightly different from the way they are on the other Channel Islands. The first noticeable difference is the fact that there is no regular ferry service to Guernsey – you have to fly with the yellow planes of *Aurigny Air Services*. Approaching the west of the island from the air, it is clear to the visitor that no precipitous coastline awaits him, as is the case on the other islands, but that the terrain slopes only very slightly upwards to the east. Some tour guides feel inclined to suggest that there is a lack of genuine tourist attractions to look forward to. Why bother going to Alderney, you may ask?

Anyone who has visited this island, which lies far out at sea, knows the reason why – and will probably want to come again and again. You can be certain that he has come to cherish not only the dazzling white beaches, lush green countryside and quiet little capital, but, above all, the island's 2,400 inhabitants.

Built in the Norman style from Alderney sandstone and Caen limestone: St Anne's Church

It is the people, with their independent character and individualistic lifestyle, who are the 'soul' of the island, and who make it so endearing. These character traits have not developed by chance, but have a lot to do with the isolation in which the islanders live. They are linked, for administrative purposes, to Guernsey – a sensible move – but there is no love lost between the two islands. For centuries, the people of Alderney kept their neighbours at arm's length and resisted all attempts to subjugate or influence them in any way. They thus secured for themselves their independent existence and developed into a lively community of self-confident individuals. It's no wonder that like-minded visitors feel so at home here.

The islanders have always felt strongly about their personal freedom and a desire for independence. In military terms, the strategically favourable position of the island in the English Channel should have made Alderney a constant bone of contention between its two powerful neighbours, England and France. This, however, has not been the case. Apart from during World War II, the tide of history has lapped only gently upon the shores of the island. One reason for this could be the fact that, over the centuries, the English have crammed the island full of military installations, more than on any of the other islands. This deterrent factor has effectively nipped any thoughts of invasion in the bud. German troops were the only ones to disturb the peace here. The inhabitants were forced to abandon their island. On their return, at the end of the war, they discovered to their horror that numerous concrete bunkers had been constructed in their absence.

During the period when the English were busy building their military installations, they left the islanders largely to their own devices. Out of an inherent sense of democracy, they granted themselves a constitution and established a small parliament. They also took every opportunity to oppose the unpopular Governors, who had been granted extensive land rights in Alderney by the English crown. This was as good a reason as any to pick a quarrel with England. As in many other places, after World War II, there was a general acceptance of the need to make a fresh start. This gave the islanders the chance to 'spring clean' the constitution, which had remained virtually unaltered for centuries. A parliamentary committee called the *States of Alderney* was set up to deal with the needs and problems of the island. It consists of 12 non-party members and the President, all of whom are elected every three years. On the whole, the system appears to work quietly and effectively, to the satisfaction of all concerned.

The numerous local pubs on the island play an important role in island communications, both amongst the islanders themselves and also between them and visitors. The people of Alderney like nothing better than a chat down at the pub – about local events, politics at Westminster and the latest cricket results. Nothing can disturb the convivial atmosphere and, in no time at all, contacts have been made that get deeper by the glass.

The island, which measures approximately 16 sq km, makes its living chiefly from tourism. More than 20,000 holidaymakers come here every year; added to this, almost half that number again come on day trips. This figure includes those who sail over from France, which lies only 12 km away. Agriculture focuses mainly on milk production; you can't beat the taste of the local *salted butter*, *vanilla ice cream* and *cheddar cheese*. Flowers are cultivated on a limited scale and are of less economic importance. Attempts are also being made to launch a financial market, similar to that on the other islands.

Alongside their *pubs* and *cricket*, the islanders love their cars. An amazing 1,500 vehicles are registered on Alderney, where even the shortest distance is covered by car, despite the fact that there are few proper roads and everything lies so close together. Consequently, it is difficult to find a parking space in town. There are no parking fees, but fixed parking times instead. In *Victoria Street*, for example, parking is restricted to one hour between 9 am and 12.30 pm and 1.30 pm and 5 pm.

Compliance with these regulations is monitored very strictly indeed by the island's two policemen. They are seconded from Guernsey every two weeks: that way they remain unbiased upholders of the law, say the islanders.

ST ANNE

(106/A-B1-2) ★ *Welcome to Alderney!* After a 15-minute flight from Guernsey, the propeller-driven planes land at the small airport, which is only 1 km away from St Anne. Passengers can reach the town either by taxi or in only ten minutes on foot.

The tiny island capital – referred to only as 'the town' – does not lie on the coast – in contrast to those on the bigger islands – but sits majestically on top of a hill in the centre of the island. ⤷ At the highest point stands the *cricket ground*, which affords a splendid view across *Braye Bay*, taking in the harbour, fortifications and beaches. From here you can also get an overall picture of the town, whose air of quiet modesty and

Alderney boasts the only railway still operating in the Channel Islands

unhurried pace makes it seem all the more charming and idyllic. Cobbled streets, narrow lanes, delicately shaded sandstone houses erected in the course of the last two centuries, interspersed with pretty, green *cottage gardens*. These visual impressions are reinforced by the convivial atmosphere of the local pubs and inns and the colourful shops. No noisy supermarkets, no neon signs – the perfect picture-postcard idyll.

The main thoroughfare is *Victoria Street*, where people and cars jockey for position – but the atmosphere is nevertheless relaxed and cheerful: no road rage here. Take the cinema, for example. It has only one modern film projector, which means that films have to be shown in two parts. Does this present a problem? Of course not. Cinemagoers use the interval to pop round to a nearby pub for a quick drink or two.

On the way down to the harbour, you come across another of the island's attractions: the only fully operational railway line in the Channel Islands. It was constructed in the middle of the 19th century to transport granite blocks from *Mannez Quarry* to the harbour. Nowadays, at the weekend, you can go for a ride in one of the two red coaches – veterans of the London Underground. Pulled by a small locomotive, the train takes you at a leisurely pace from *Braye Beach* to *Longis Beach.*

SIGHTS

Braye Harbour   (106/B1)
★ A ten-minute walk through the lush vegetation of *Petit Val* takes you down to the harbour. This somewhat sleepy-looking port is characterized by its 18th-century warehouses, a row of handsome buildings – including numerous pubs – and a 1,500-m-long mole stretching out into the sea. The *breakwater* was built in the mid-19th century to lessen the impact of the thundering waves that crash onto the land in stormy weather. Originally it was intended that the harbour and fortress should be extended to form part of a defensive cordon against the French. The plans, however, got no further than the drawing board. ❖ Today's main attraction are the traditional pubs, full of character and maritime charm, with their magnificent pub signs hanging outside. Each one deserves a visit – we suggest you work your way through them one at a time!

Island Hall   (106/B2)
The former Governor's residence is the No. 1 address for social gatherings on the island, hosting many big events. Entertainment stars generally begin their tours of the Channel Islands here, you could say as a sort of dress rehearsal. The building also houses the library and bowling alley. Holiday guests are of course most welcome.

Marais Square   (106/B2)
The square was originally the heart of the village, where, amongst other things, cattle auctions were held. A historic livestock drinking trough still stands here today, with, logically enough, a human watering place, the *Pub Marais* in the background. Several of the old houses in the *venelles*, the side streets of *Le Huret* quarter, survive today. Every year on New Year's Day, the island's firemen get together on

The Alderney Museum in St Anne gives an insight into the island's history

Marais Square for their traditional, convivial water extravaganza.

Old Bell Tower (106/B2)
A popular subject amongst photographers, this tower is all that remains of the former village church, whose clock stood still one day at 5.11. At its foot is the old graveyard with its time-worn headstones. *Highstreet*

St Anne's Church (106/B2)
The church, built in 1850, is a real architectural gem and is regarded affectionately by the islanders as the *Cathedral of the Channel Islands*. The architectural style of the church is clearly influenced by the Normans, not least because it is built from limestone imported from Caen. The modern glass windows contrast well with the style of the building. The peaceful atmosphere inside the church is echoed outside in the graveyard with its weathered headstones and fine old trees. *Victoria Street*

States Offices (106/B2)
This is the seat of government in Alderney. The conference chamber of the island parliament is located on the first floor. The building also houses the law court, the police station and the tourist office. Court sessions are held every Thursday, when the judge flies in from Guernsey to pass judgement and – very occasionally – sentence a law-breaker to a spell in the island's two-cell prison. Up until the end of the 18th century, trials were held in the open in *Connaught Square, Queen Elizabeth II Street*

Alderney Museum (106/B2)
The former school house is home to a simple but effective exhibition of items that have been lov-

ingly put together to illustrate the history of the island from prehistoric times, via the *liberation* from German Occupation down to the present day. The museum also offers a wealth of information on local flora and fauna and on life in the mudflats and the waters around the island. You really should make a point of seeing this highly original collection. *High Street; Mon–Fri 10 am–noon and 2 pm–4 pm; June–Aug also Sat–Sun 10 am–noon; free admission, though a small donation is expected*

RESTAURANTS

First & Last
A small, excellent fish restaurant, whose name is derived from the fact that, whichever way you approach it, its the first and last house on the island. *Braye Street; Tel. 82 31 62; category 2*

The Georgian House
As the name suggests, this restaurant is located in a Georgian-style building and is noted for the stylish presentation of its fresh fish dishes. The pub has good beer on tap. *The Garden Beyond* offers first-rate light meals. *Victoria Street; Tel. 82 24 71; category 2*

Nellie Gray's Restaurant
Fantastic French cuisine in an elegant restaurant – evenings only, though. *Victoria Street; Tel. 82 33 33; category 1*
   Nellie Gray's Garden is a cosy beer garden serving traditional meals and drinks. Open all day. *Category 2*

Rose & Crown Inn
☩ Come on a Friday and be sure to try the *fish'n'chips* with mushy peas! The rest of the menu is no less traditional in flavour. The beer garden is especially popular with a young clientele. The *Wine Shop* in the cellar has a good selection of fine wines. *Le Huret; Tel. 82 34 14; category 3*

SHOPPING

Alderney Pottery
This out-of-the-way pottery is a favourite meeting place for crafts enthusiasts. Here, you can look around and buy, drink tea and try the home-made cake. Holidaymakers can also take part in pottery courses. *Les Mouriaux; Mon–Fri 9 am–5 pm, Sat 9 am–1 pm, Sun 2 pm–5 pm*

Arte Fina
Gallery specializing in beautiful Alderney watercolours. *At the corner of Victoria Street and High Street; Mon–Sat 10.30 am–1 pm and 4 pm–6 pm*

The Stamp Shop
The Post Office has a wide selection of Alderney postage stamps and coins. *Victoria Street; 9 am–12.30 pm and 1.30 pm–5 pm*

Victoria Antiques
This dealer stocks mainly Victorian silverware, but also jewellery and porcelain. *Victoria Street; Mon–Sat 10 am–12.30 pm and 4 pm–6 pm*

ACCOMMODATION

Chez André
Popular, most agreeable hotel with fine restaurant and pretty café on the terrace. *17 rooms; Victoria Street; Tel. 82 27 77; Fax 82 29 62; category 2*

Inchalla
Modern hotel, standing on the outskirts of town towards the

harbour. Regarded as the best hotel on the island, it also has a very good restaurant. *11 rooms; The Val; Tel. 82 32 20; Fax 82 35 51; category 1*

Rose & Crown

Here you'll find a number of pleasant, reasonably priced rooms above the restaurant. *6 rooms; Le Huret; Tel. 82 34 14; Fax 82 36 15; category 3*

Sea View Hotel

Stylish hotel with its own good restaurant. Ideally situated for beach-lovers, since it is just a stone's throw away from *Braye Beach. 16 rooms; Braye Street; Tel. 82 27 38; Fax 82 35 72; category 2*

SPORTS & LEISURE

The island offers a wide range of sporting activities. *Alderney Tourism Services* has further information. Important contact addresses and telephone numbers:

Water sports: the sea around Alderney is very popular sailing and yachting territory. The *Alderney Sailing Club (Tel. 82 29 59)* readily welcomes guests. The beaches are ideal for water-skiing and windsurfing.

Tennis: courts are available at all times at the *Alderney Tennis Club (Tel. 82 32 12).*

Golf: the island boasts a nine-hole course, which is open to visiting players. *Alderney Golf Club (Tel. 82 28 35)*

A Mecca for keen sandcastle builders: Braye Bay

ENTERTAINMENT

♪ There are no discos as such on the island. Look out, though, for notices of forthcoming events at the *Chez Bar* in *Victoria Street*. An all-time favourite evening pastime amongst locals and holiday guests is *pub jumping*: great atmosphere and fun guaranteed!

INFORMATION

Tourism Information Centre
Victoria Street; Mon–Fri 10 am–noon and 2 pm–4 pm, Sat 10 am–noon; Tel. 82 37 37; Fax 82 24 36

SURROUNDING AREA

Braye Bay (106/B1)
★ This picturesque bay is the site of the island's No. 1 beach. Its proximity to the town and harbour mean that it is often quite crowded. Children in particular love paddling and building sandcastles here. 1 km

Burhou Island (O)
To the west of Alderney, on a rock that is only 1 km long and half a kilometre wide, is the protected breeding ground of the famous puffin. Ornithologists may visit the island outside the breeding season *(March–July; contact the Harbour Office for more information; Tel. 82 26 20).* 5 km

Château à L'Etoc (106/C1)
The fort stands on the northernmost tip of the island, on a prehistoric site. Like the 12 similar structures on Alderney, it was built from 1847 to 1855 by Captain William Jervois. To the east of the Château lie the ruins of *Fort Les Homeaux Florains* and

Fort Houmet Herbé with *Fort Quesnard* in between. 2 km

These coastal fortifications were erected to protect against invasion. They have not only been able to fulfil their military purpose, but also their architectural form blends well into the island landscape. This becomes particularly apparent if you take a boat trip around the island. It is even possible to ignore the ugly, concrete bunkers that were added onto the forts at the time of the Occupation. Most of the forts are now privately owned and have been converted into holiday apartments.

Corblets Bay (106/C1)
Between cliffs, the bay's sandy beach is an ideal spot for swimming. At the eastern end stands *Fort Corblets*, a handsome fort made from reddish sandstone. 3 km

Essex Castle (106/C2)
The fortress on the edge of the cliffs dominates *Longis Bay* below. 2 km

This is also the start of an impressive cliff-top path that winds its way along the 5 km to *Hannaine Bay*, taking in the intriguing rock formations of the south and west coasts. A 'must' for the adventurous hiker.

Fort Albert (106/B1)
This mighty and imposing fortress dominates the eastern end of Braye Bay. It was built in the Victorian era to defend the harbour. Only the protective outer walls remain today, on the north and west sides. Dotted about amongst the ruins are concrete blocks, remnants of the German Occupation, which add a sinister note to the atmosphere of the site. ☙
The fabulous panorama reaching

as far as Crabby Bay and Fort Doyle is most impressive. 1.5 km

Fort Clonque (106/A2)

〰 This compact, restored fortress braves the waters on a picturesque spot off the west coast between *Clonque Bay* and *Hannaine Bay*. The rocky island on which it stands is accessible by car via a causeway. From here, there is also a good view over to *Fort Tourgis*, the barracks complex on the other side of the bay. 2 km

Les Etacs (106/A2)

Alderney's most westerly point lies 300 m out to sea. The group of islands known as *Les Etacs* is home to a colony of sea birds. Some 1,500 screeching pairs of gannets appear to drown the cliff face in a sea of white, tightly huddled together on their precarious footholds. Take a pair of binoculars, or better still, treat yourself to a round trip of the island by boat for an even better view. 3 km

Lighthouse (106/C1)

The 32-m-high lighthouse, which was built in 1912, is clearly visible to all passing ships and, thanks to its deafening foghorn, not to be overheard! It stands on the north coast of the island *(for guided tours, contact the Tourism Information Centre)*. 3 km

The lighthouses on Guernsey and Sark and also the warning light on an unmanned lightship in the Channel are controlled via computer from *Alderney Lighthouse*.

The waters around Alderney are extremely dangerous. The tidal range of 11 m is so great that the water flowing past the island is thrust with such force that two powerful currents are generated, *the Swinge* around the north

coast and *the Race* to the south. Both have been the cause of many a shipwreck in the past and are feared amongst sailors even today.

Longis Bay (106/C1)

Situated on the north coast, this beautiful bay with its long, white beach has one shortcoming: the anti-tank wall, erected during the last war, that skirts the bay makes a rather ugly backdrop.

★ On the *Ile de Raz*, in the middle of the bay, stands *Fort Raz*, which can be reached on foot via a causeway at low tide. 〰 From here there is a terrific view south towards the breathtaking cliff formations known as the *Hanging Rocks*. 2 km

Saye Bay (106/C1)

Sheltered from the wind, this bay with its fine, sandy beach is situated on the north coast. Nearby is the island's camp site. 2 km

The Nunnery (106/C1)

Ancient remains of walls of unknown origin have been discovered near Longis Bay. They could possibly have been part of a Norman settlement. The islanders refer to them disrespectfully as the 'Nunnery', whereby they don't actually mean nuns, but rather the 'ladies' they associate with the soldiers stationed at Essex Castle during the Napoleonic period! 2 km

War Memorial (106/C1)

The marble monument is always decorated with fresh flowers. The inscription on its plaque is a tribute written in six languages to the slave labourers who died while building the island's many concrete bunkers and anti-tank defences during World War II. 1 km

Horse-drawn carriages and bicycles

Nature beats the rhythm and the island follows –
accompanied only by the rumbling of tractor engines

Although it is sometimes rather choppy, visitors have seldom cause to regret embarking on the crossing from Guernsey to Sark. The boat of The *Isle of Sark Shipping Company* takes 40 minutes for the 14 km that separate both islands. With each kilometre, the beauty of Sark's coastline becomes more apparent, with its deeply fissured, craggy cliffs and, from a distance, it is possible to make out rocky pillars and jagged archways framing the entrances to fantastic caves. The 120-m-high cliff face is broken up by picturesque sand and pebble bays, where sailing boats and yachts ride at anchor. What a picture!

Measuring approximately 5 km in length and 2.5 km in width, the island is larger than Herm, but small enough for you to get to know it in the space of a day trip. There are, however, a number of very well-appointed hotels, should you be tempted to stay longer. And there are reasons enough to do so: not only the

The prestigious seat of the Seigneur of Sark: La Seigneurie on Great Sark

many beautiful spots and natural attractions on the island, but also its peaceful, quiet atmosphere. 'Quiet' up to a point, that is. There may be no cars on Sark, but this fact is more than made up for by the roaring and clattering tractors. It was not long ago that only two of them were in use on the island. In the meantime, every family has its own tractor and makes loud use of it!

The obligation to keep the island as far as possible noise-free, is self-imposed. Over 400 years ago, Sark drew up its own 'constitution', the basic principles of which are not only still valid but are actively implemented today. The island – all 8 sq km of it – is therefore the smallest independent state within the United Kingdom and its 600 or so inhabitants are the subjects of the last feudal administration in Europe. The founder of this unique state structure was Hélier de Carteret, who freed the island in 1564 from short-lived French occupation. As a reward – and for the price of £40 – he was granted the island as a fiefdom by the English crown. He thus became the first *Seigneur* of Sark. As a distinctly dem-

MARCO POLO SELECTION: SARK

1 La Coupée
This ridge breathtakingly links both Sark islands (page 85)

2 La Seigneurie Gardens
Exotic plants en masse, with a wonderful view of La Seigneurie (page 84)

3 The Window
The attraction above *Port du Moulin* bay is a manmade breach in the

cliffs, offering an amazing panorama (page 86)

4 La Sablonnerie Hotel
The 400-year-old cottage houses a romantic hotel and a pleasant restaurant (page 86)

5 Venus Pool
The rock pools and whispering cave Gorey Souffleur: two impressive natural wonders (page 87)

ocratic thinker, he divided the island up amongst the 40 settlers. These owners of the so-called *tenements* were entitled to one vote each in the *Chief Pleas*. They were now members of what was to all intents and purposes a parliamentary assembly, which met three times a year under the chairmanship of the Seigneur. On these occasions, they passed laws, in accordance with the then valid Norman legal code. The Seigneur had a limited right of veto, whereby he could not block altogether the resolutions made by the majority, but only delay their coming into force. Voting rights attached to each *tenement* passed down the centuries from father to son, and the *Chief Pleas* still exists in this form today.

In 1924, it was decided that 12 new members should be admitted to the assembly, who had been elected democratically by the island population. What we see today is an intact island community with healthy finances, despite its low tax rates. The most important source of income are the harbour dues, which are included in the price of each ferry ticket sold to visitors, who come in such numbers that tourism has advanced to become the most lucrative sector of the economy. It's no surprise that each guest is made particularly welcome.

Visitors can explore the central plateau on a romantic ride in a horse-drawn carriage. The ideal means of transport on the island is, without a doubt, the bicycle; consequently in the high season it can be difficult to get hold of one of the 1,200 that are available for hire. However, it is also possible to take in the astonishing variety of idyllic island landscapes on foot – even though there is no designated route along the 65 km of coastline.

At low tide, the inviting bays with their sandy or pebble beaches are great for swimming and sunbathing, although the climb down – and back up again – via seemingly endless flights of steps can be a bit off-putting. If you intend spending a few hours down in the bays, it's well worth the effort of getting there. When you do, you are more than compensated by the crystal-clear water and absolute peace and solitude you'll find waiting for you.

GREAT SARK

(106/B-C4-5) Boats put in on the east coast of the island at *La Maseline Harbour*, Sark's main harbour. Tractors with trailers are waiting to take visitors up the steep *Harbour Hill* to the village. For those who prefer to walk, a romantic, overgrown woodland path runs parallel to the road. Once up in the square, *La Colinette*, you can take a seat in one of the carriages or hire a bicycle for the next leg of your trip.

Less than 100 m away, *the Avenue* begins, the village shopping street. The road is lined with single-storey houses containing several shops, which stock all sorts of more or less useful items. Halfway along is the Post Office and Sark's only post box. Close by is also the island's tiny prison, with room to accommodate two prisoners – should there ever be any. Next door is the *Senior School*, the seat of the island parliament, and the Gothic granite church of *St Peter* built in 1820, with its modern glass windows.

SIGHTS

Creux Harbour　　　　(106/C5)
This snug little anchorage lies directly adjacent to *La Maseline*, the main harbour. It was constructed by the first settlers in the 16th century and can be reached only via a tunnel. Once a year, in summer, when the tide is favourable, *Water Carnival Sunday* is held here, with fun and games in and on the water, for young and old.

The most comfortable way to discover the small island

La Seigneurie (106/B4)

One kilometre to the north of the village stands La Seigneurie, on the site of a sixth-century priory that was demolished in the Middle Ages. This impressive manor house, begun in the mid-16th century, has served as the prestigious seat of the Seigneur since 1730. Each successive owner has left his distinctive mark on the building, adding new architectural features, which has resulted in a somewhat incoherent whole. Even the powerful-looking tower, built in 1854 and the last addition to the building, cannot rectify this overall impression. Nor did it ever fulfil its original function, namely to allow the sending of light signals from Sark to Guernsey; there was never any cause to do so. The manor house is not open to the public. Behind the house is the interesting dovecote and six bronze cannons, amongst which stands a German artillery gun, which somehow found its way here during World War II. ★ Visitors can stroll around the park and *La Seigneurie Gardens*, surrounded by high walls and filled with exotic flowers. *Easter–Oct, Mon–Fri 10 am–5 pm; admission: 80 p*

Windmill (106/B4)

〰️ On the western edge of the village, crowning the highest point on the island (120 m), stands an old windmill, dating from the year 1571. Today it houses a souvenir shop and is a pretty subject for a photograph.

ACCOMMODATION

Dixcart Hotel (106/B5)

Victor Hugo once stayed in this former feudal manor house and was impressed by the beautiful park-like gardens and nearby *Dixcart Bay*. The restaurant is noted

The causeway between Great Sark and Little Sark, La Coupée

Community spirit

Sark is still governed today like a medieval state. There are laws, of course, but many decisions are made in accordance with traditional principles of common law. There is, for example, no health insurance and no national insurance to pay the unemployed. If a resident falls on hard times, he is given help according to the principle of reciprocity: a jointly held fund covers any costs incurred. In this way, no one must live in fear of getting into serious difficulties.

for its fine cuisine. *19 rooms; Tel. 83 20 15; Fax 83 21 64; category 2*

La Moinerie   (106/B4)

This charming renovated farmhouse, built in 1728, stands in a tranquil spot in a wooded valley close to La Seigneurie. The delicious lobster from the waters around the island is the house speciality. *9 rooms; Tel. 83 20 89; Fax 83 24 59; category 2*

Petit Champ   (106/B4)

Secluded location amidst lush greenery, close to the west coast. Peaceful country-house atmosphere. Good restaurant serving fresh fish and seafood. *16 rooms; Tel. 83 20 46; Fax 83 24 69; category 2*

ENTERTAINMENT

The evenings here are quiet. The hotel pubs are the place to go to meet people. ✱ On Tuesday and Saturday evenings there is a disco at the *Mermaid Tavern* for young guests.

SURROUNDING AREA

Brecqhou   (106/A4)

This 40-hectare island slumbers peacefully on the other side of the 70-m-wide *Gouliot Passage*, which divides it from the west coast of Sark. However, since it is privately owned and may not be visited, the natural delights of the island can only be guessed at.

Dixcart Bay   (106/B5)

Easily accessible and a popular place to swim at low tide. The bay is situated in the south of Great Sark, flanked by spectacular cliff formations. On the left, the steep-sided *Hog's Back* peninsula juts out into the sea. On the other side of this headland is *Derrible Bay* with its equally lovely sandy beach. Here, cave enthusiasts will discover a natural monument: the 60-m-deep *Creux du Derrible*, one of the many caves on the island, and certainly the most beautiful.

La Coupée   (106/B5)

★ ◁◁▷ Great Sark and Little Sark are joined together by a narrow ridge, some 78 m high. Crossing it is quite an experience. In the days before German prisoners of war reinforced the roadway after the last war, it was almost impossible to cross from one part of the island to the other in stormy weather. Even today, cyclists wanting to cross over are required to get off and push, for safety reasons. ◁◁▷ The reward for this tightrope-like stunt is a breathtaking view across the sea to the neighbouring islands.

Port du Moulin (106/B4)

On the west coast, close to *La Seigneurie*, is this easily accessible bay, which served monks as a harbour in the seventh century. The monks cut a terrace into the rock face, some 75 m above ground. From here, they were able, with the aid of a block and tackle, to unload boats and harvest seaweed to be used as fertilizer on their fields. In the 19th century the then Seigneur had a passageway cut out of the rock for the same purpose. ★ ✹ *The Window*, as it is called, gives the visitor what can only be described as a sensational panoramic view and is therefore one of the major attractions on any island tour.

LITTLE SARK

(106/B5-6) It is surely only a matter of time before the waters of *Grande Gréve Bay* have gnawed their way through *La Coupée* to finally sever the link between the two Sark islands. A bridge will span the resulting strait, in place of today's narrow causeway, although people are generally reluctant to think this far into the future. One thing is certain, though: it would do nothing to diminish the natural charm of this peaceful, idyllic island.

The terrain here on Little Sark is similar to that of her 'big sister': a plateau with steep cliffs falling away on all sides. The island is just 1,500 m long and 900 m wide. Lush green pastures, dotted with cows grazing contentedly, are interrupted by only a handful of minor roads. These lead to the old farms *La Sablonnerie*, *La Pipeterie*, *La Duvallerie*, *La Moderie* and *La Donellerie*, which lie loosely grouped around a spring. This is also where the roadway from *La Coupée* ends.

SIGHTS

La Clôture (106/B6)

At the end of the road lies *La Clôture*, site of a barracks used in the Napoleonic Wars. The cannon that stands on the edge of the cliff harks back to this period.

Silver mine (106/B6)

Close by *La Clôture* stand the overgrown and dilapidated ventilation shafts of the disused silver mine. In 1834, veins of silver were discovered here, and it was decided to tunnel beneath the seabed to exploit them. The 'silver rush', however, ended in disaster. A ship carrying the entire yield sank on the way to England and, in a second incident, an underwater tunnel collapsed; ten miners drowned in the ensuing flood. Investments to the value of £30,000 were irrevocably lost and the mining venture was abandoned.

ACCOMMODATION

La Sablonnerie Hotel (106/B5)

★ The hotel in the 400-year-old cottage radiates an irresistible charm. It is regarded as the best on the island, a fact that is readily confirmed by those who have had the pleasure of staying or just eating there. *22 rooms; Tel. 83 20 61; Fax 83 24 08; category 1*

Whether indoors, in the cosy rooms with their warming fireplaces or outside on the flower-filled terrace or even in the *La Sablonnerie Tea Garden,* you can't help but feel at home. Added to this, the dishes conjured up in the

A 400-year-old cottage: La Sablonnerie Hotel on Little Sark

kitchen from ingredients taken fresh from the garden or the waters round about are a delight to the palate. *Tel. 83 20 61; category 2*

SURROUNDING AREA

Adonis Pool (106/A5)

The adventurous visitor can climb down from *Adonis Headland* on the west coast and be rewarded, at low tide, with a swim in the crystal-clear water of this natural pool.

La Grande Grève (106/B5)

At the foot of *La Coupée*, down some 300 uneven steps, is what Sark-lovers consider to be the most beautiful bay on the island: La Grande Grève, with its glorious sandy beach.

A paradise for surfers and wind-surfers alike, when the waves crash onto the shore. A walk along the coast at low tide reveals interesting cliff formations and caves, such as *La Chapelle* and *Les Epines*.

Venus Pool (106/B6)

★ Between Platrue Bay and Clouet Bay in the south lie the natural rock pools, which go to make up the 10-m-wide and almost 6-m-deep Venus Pool. At low tide, it sits high and dry between the rocky cliffs, filled with glorious warm water, just right for swimming, its edge decorated with sea anemones. In *Platrue Bay* is the largest of three caves, the whispering cavern known as *Gorey Souffleur*. Since the cave vault is higher than the entrance, the incoming waves produce strange, heart-rending sounds. Great jets of water are forced out when the waters are sucked out again.

A byword for contentedness

Peace and natural beauty cast a spell on the visitor, transporting him to a quieter world

No holiday guest on Guernsey should miss the opportunity to visit the little island of Herm, surrounded by deep blue water and a mere 20 minutes by boat from St Peter Port. It may be only 2 sq km in size, but its natural beauty and individual charm more than compensate for this. Herm is a haven of tranquillity, undisturbed by the sound of roaring exhaust pipes or blaring transistor radios. The tenant of the island has decreed that peace shall reign – and so it does.

Since 1949 Major Peter Wood has headed this somewhat feudal society, then as now with a strong sense of responsibility and wise far-sightedness. All the island's public facilities belong to him, from the power supply to the kindergarten, likewise all commercial businesses, such as the farm or the souvenir shop. Everything operates in a well-ordered fashion and flourishes quite respectably. He is therefore in a position not only to exploit the unique features of the island, but also to care for them and develop them further.

Romantic country house on Herm

The countryside of Herm is outstandingly beautiful. In the north, the land is fairly flat and fabulous beaches tempt the visitor to go for a swim. The steeply sloping south, on the other hand, boasts romantic cliff-top paths, ideal for walking. In between, an idyllic landscape of lush, green meadows where over 100 Guernsey cows graze and pose quite unassumingly for photographers.

A complete tour of the island takes around 90 minutes, so even a half-day trip is sufficient to take in all the highlights. Ferries ply between Guernsey and Herm up to eight times per day. Those who manage to catch the 8.30 am *milk boat* can also witness the delivery of supplies to the island.

HARBOUR VILLAGE

(104/A1) It would of course be an exaggeration to call the small cluster of houses around the harbour pier a town: a small village would be more appropriate. The pale blue and pink houses around the square, which is called the *Piazza*, do make a pretty, homely picture. They house shops, pubs and holiday flats. The only building that lends the village a touch of city atmosphere is the former prison, which now stands in the garden of the hotel. It was big enough to accommodate just one prisoner.

SIGHTS

Belvoir Bay   (104/A-B1)
This small, quiet bay, nestling beneath the cliffs of the east coast, is very popular with swimmers. The beach café, which stands above, it is also a good place to take a break on your round trip of the island.

Manor House   (104/A1)
In the centre of the island, hidden behind an enclosing wall, is the tenant's estate, which dates from the 15th century. The dominant feature is the crenellated tower. That is just about all you can see, since the house itself is not open to the public. ★ Also on the estate is the 17th-century *St Tugual's Chapel*, which may be visited. This small, granite church with its colourful stained-glass windows was built by Benedictine monks

from Mont St Michel. It has survived down the centuries and was delightfully renovated after the war. A service is held each Sunday morning.

Point Sauzebourge   (104/A2)
★ ⇘ High above the south-west tip of the island, as you stand on the path along the cliffs, the panoramic view is tremendous. Straight ahead out to sea lies the tiny island of *Jethou*, surrounded by countless islets and reefs. Dotted in between are colourful boats against the deep blue of the sea. Stretched out away in the distance, the east coast of Guernsey is visible.

Jethou is known to be blessed with lush vegetation and colourful flowers, especially hyacinths and cowslips. Unfortunately, the delights of the island must remain an object for speculation, since the owner allows no visitors.

Robert's Cross Dolmen   (104/A1)
On a low hill behind the expanse of sand known as *Mouissonnière Beach* stands an obelisk, visible for miles around and therefore a point of reference for passing

Up to 150 types of sea shell get washed up on Shell Beach, Herm

MARCO POLO SELECTION: HERM

1 Shell Beach
A beach at the northern end of the east coast, popular amongst shell-collecting enthusiasts (page 91)

2 St Tugual's Chapel
On the estate of the island tenant, who often holds services himself (page 90)

3 Point Sauzebourge
A marvellous panorama from the cliff-top path high above the south-west tip (page 90)

4 The White House Hotel
A refined hotel, reflecting every aspect of the island's charm (page 91)

ships. It was constructed from stones gathered from the remains of several 4,000-year-old graves. Nearby is *Robert's Cross*, the largest grave, measuring 6 m in length.

Rosière Steps   (104/A1)
At low tide, it is not possible for ships to berth at the harbour pier. Therefore, they put in at *Rosière Steps* a little farther south, on the west coast. This staircase, framed with cheerful, white stone with a granite archway, is also a pleasant spot to while away the time, doing nothing in particular except to enjoy the view.

Shell Beach   (104/A1)
★ Laid out, as if on a silver salver, along the northern end of the east coast is this beautiful, almost 1-km-long beach. First and foremost, it is an eldorado for families with a passion for collecting shells, since the Gulf Stream delivers a constant supply of exotic sea shells, up to 150 different types at the last count. A pleasant beach café serves snacks and refreshments.

RESTAURANTS

Captain's Table Coffee Shop
The house speciality are the famous and delicious Herm oysters. The rest of the seafood menu also comes highly recommended. *Category 2*

Mermaid Tavern
Although they are used to catering for the masses here, the food in the garden café is good and reasonably priced. The drinks come from the pub. *Tel. 71 01 70; category 3*

The Ship Restaurant
✪ Pub with terrace, sophisticated drinks and light meals. *Tel. 72 21 59; category 2*

ACCOMMODATION

The White House Hotel   (104/A1)
★ This hotel, in a dazzling white country house can be seen from the ship as you approach the island. Its facilities include a well-tended garden, a swimming pool and a tennis court. The restaurant prides itself on its excellent cuisine. *38 rooms; Tel. 72 23 77; Fax 71 00 66; category 1*

Right round the islands

These routes are marked in green on the map on the inside front cover and in the Road Atlas beginning on page 104

① JERSEY

The island is small enough to allow you to discover its historical sights and many beautiful rural spots in one day, if you take a car. Should you have seen enough of the small island capital, St Helier, you are sure to have worked up an appetite for the rest of the island. Choose a sunny day, jump in the car early and look forward to your day trip of around 65 km.

The starting point in St Helier is *Victoria Avenue*, which leads you directly into the semicircular *St Aubin's Bay* (page 45). The prelude is in *St Aubin* (page 45), the prettiest little town on the island. Stop for a while on the harbour promenade and stroll out to the rocky island lying just offshore, on which stands *St Aubin's Fort* (page 45). From here you can enjoy the magnificent view across the bay to the idyllic *Elizabeth Castle* (pages 35–36), basking in the morning sunshine. Back at the harbour, you will enjoy the sight of the row of pubs huddled up next to each other. It's too early for a drink, though you can make up for this on a future visit – you're bound to come again, since here in St Aubin begins the famous *Corbière Walk* (page 45), a fixed item on any Jersey itinerary. Follow the winding road

up onto the plateau and turn into the *Route de Noirmont*. The road ends, high above a breathtaking cliff face, at *Noirmont Point* (page 46), which offers you the promised beautiful outlook over land and sea. At the foot of the cliffs is *Portelet Bay* (page 47), which can be reached only by climbing narrow flights of steps. This charming cove is an obvious choice for a lazy day at the beach at some point later in your holiday. Next stop is *St Brelade's Bay* (page 47), the island's ever-popular holiday paradise. Skirted by exotic plants and Mediterranean trees, this superlative beach gives you everything you'd expect from an island summer holiday. You could make an enjoyable detour to *Beau Port* (page 46), a secluded cove, featuring the smallest beach on the south coast. Only a few kilometres separate you now from magnificent *La Corbière* (page 46). Amidst the treacherous rocks, lashed by the waves, stands a white lighthouse on an offshore islet, marking Jersey's south-west tip. The view northwards in the direction of *St Ouen's Bay* (page 51) prepares you for the next stage of the journey. This playground for young and old offers ideal conditions for many sporting activities, such as sand racing on the beach and surfing in the waves, which thunder onto the shore. In the dunes behind the beach lies *Mielle de Morville (page 51)*. In *Kempt Tower*, the Martello tower on the coast road, you can find out more about the nature reserve. Up on the plateau above, you'll find the ruins of *Grosnez Castle (page 51)*. There is a terrific view from here of wild and stormy *Grosnez Point (page 51)* amidst the *Paternoster Rocks (page 51)*, dreaded by mariners. Far from the main tourist routes, the cliff-top paths of the north coast are a peaceful haven for the rambler with an eye for nature. A good example is the path to the *Col de la Rocque*. Following on from this is the pleasant drive to *Plémont Point (page 51)*, towering over *Plémont Bay (page 51)*, which is neatly enclosed by the sheer cliffs. Should you arrive at high tide, though, you won't see much of the idyllic bay itself. *Grève le Lecq (pages 50–51)* boasts the oldest Martello tower on the island and, with *Le Moulin de Lecq (page 51)*, can offer a lunch-time stopover full of character. The massive water wheel at this 600-year-old mill still turns to this day. Refreshment is strongly recommended at this point, since the next stop is the *Devil's Hole (pages 49–50)*. The climb down – and back up again – can be quite exhausting. Take a well-earned rest on a detour to the nearby *La Mare Vineyards (page 49)*, the only wine-growing area in the Channel Islands. Near the coast, close to *St John's Village*, begins yet another footpath along the coast to *Rozel Bay (page 44)*. This stretch is for hikers only, since the road turns back inland, and only returns to the coast at *Rozel (page 44)*. This little fishing village sits snugly in the bay and is regarded by many

keen Jersey fans as one of the most beautiful places on the island. After a wander round the village, don't forget to drop in at homely *Apple Cottage Restaurant (page 44)* for afternoon tea. The road along the east coast brings you back within reach of the sea. *St Catherine's Bay (page 44)* is the first of a string of endlessly long sweeps of sand. The dominant feature of Gorey is *Mont Orgueil Castle (page 42)*, standing proudly above the fishing village. The most impressive route up to the castle takes you up the flight of steps behind the row of houses on the quayside. The higher you climb, the more spectacular the view! Back in the village, we recommend a visit to *Jersey Pottery (page 43)*. The adjoining restaurant is noted for its fish dishes and is a Mecca for lovers of fine food. The drive along the sandy beach at the *Royal Bay of Grouville (page 44)* finally takes you to *Rocque Point*, the south-eastern tip of the island. At low tide, the south coast reveals its strange and fascinating rocky landscape, which can be best appreciated from the headland known as *Green Island (page 42)*. Following the beach, *La Grève d'Azette (page 42)*, you return to St Helier, where an evening in a friendly pub or an elegant restaurant brings the day to an agreeable close.

② GUERNSEY

 Both of the larger Channel Islands seem to have many common characteristics, especially when it comes to planning a round-trip of each island. However, as is so often the case, appearances can be deceptive. On closer inspection, you will see that Guernsey has very much its own special character, with cultural and scenic attractions to match! Since the overall route is shorter and

the points of interest lie closer together, you can easily afford to take your time when exploring and sightseeing or when stopping for a break in between. Total length of the day trip: approximately 40 km.

As you take your leave of *St Peter Port* for your day trip round the island, take one last look at *Castle Cornet (pages 55–56)* glowing in the morning sun. On the southern outskirts of the town is *Fort George (page 60)*, where you can wander around and imagine what it would be like to live in this idyllic setting amongst the island's millionaires. Back on your original course, you take the road through the lush, green vegetation along the east coast, before making your first detour of the day to *Fermain Bay (page 68)*, the most attractive bay on the island. Fermain Bay is a byword amongst nature-lovers, since this is the start of a uniquely beautiful footpath along the exhilarating south coast. If you wish to explore the many pretty coves below the steep cliffs, you must do so on foot; none is accessible by car. To gain a true impression of the beauty of this fascinating landscape, you should go along to *St Martin's Point (page 21)*, marking the extreme south-east of the island. It takes a certain amount of patience to discover the points of access to the bays, which lie to the west of St Martin's Point, namely *Moulin Huet Bay (page 68)* and *Petit Bôt Bay (page 69)*. Rest assured, your efforts will be rewarded, for these bathing highlights are amongst the major attractions on the island. Carrying on, take the route that leads inland through the rural parish of *Torteval (page 21)*, which extends across the plain. Only now and again is it possible to catch a glimpse over the edge of the cliffs and out to sea.

The south-west corner of the island, culminating in the *Pleinmont Point (page 62)*, is somewhat barren and bleak. The adjacent stretch of west coast encloses the crescent-shaped *Rocquaine Bay (page 62)* with its endless, sandy beaches. The most striking feature of the bay is the white Martello tower *Fort Grey (page 62)*. Today, it is home to the island's *Maritime Museum (page 61)*, which documents, amongst other things, the history of the many ships that have run aground on the hazardous coast. Lying just off the north-west corner of the island is *Lihou Island (pages 61–62)*. On it stand the sparse remains of the medieval *Priory of St Mary (page 60)*. This rocky island can be reached only when the tide is out, via an ancient causeway. A more interesting object for a visit is the *L'Erée peninsula (pages 61–62)*. Here you will find the prehistoric monuments *Trépied Dolmen (page 62)* and *Le Creux ès Faies (page 62)*. Unfortunately, nearby *Fort Saumarez (page 62)* is not accessible to visitors, since it is in private ownership. The north coast is a paradise for swimmers and other water-sports enthusiasts: a chain of bays, one after the other. They offer ideal conditions for all kinds of surfing activities. Things get off to a pleasant start at pretty *Perelle Bay*, from where we recommend you make a short detour to the chapel of *Ste Apolline (pages 62–63)*. This dates from the Middle Ages and is certainly an architectural treasure of the island and well worth seeing. *Vazon Bay (page 60)* and *Cobo Bay (page 60)* are famous not only for their lovely sandy beaches, but also as vantage points to marvel at the terrific sunset panoramas. In the northern part of the island,

L'Ancresse Bay (pages 64–65) is guarded by six watchtowers and enclosed by the 18-hole golf course. Hidden away at the fifth hole, you'll discover the prehistoric burial chambers *Les Fouaillages (page 65)* and *Varde Dolmen (page 65)*. A similar, impressive monument is the *Déhus Dolmen (page 65)*, set in a heavenly spot at the end of a tiny, narrow road. On the way, you pass *Beaucette Marina (page 64)*, a tiny harbour cut into the rock, where ocean-going yachts ride at anchor, gently bobbing up and down on the waves. *Vale Castle (page 65)*, which stands just outside St Sampson Harbour, is a good place to admire the splendid view of the entire harbour area and the east coast stretching far into the distance. The road continues, closely following the rocky *Belle Grève Bay (page 63)*, back to St Peter Port.

③ ALDERNEY

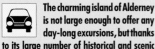

The charming island of Alderney is not large enough to offer any day-long excursions, but thanks to its large number of historical and scenic attractions, it's well worth your while spending even half a day here. Many beautiful bays await you plus a total of 14 impressive fortresses – one picture postcard image after the other! Total length of the route: 14 km.

Before you set off, don't forget to stop off at the *cricket ground (page 73)* in *St Anne (page 73)* – lovingly called the *'town'* by its inhabitants. From here the panoramic view of the island and surrounding sea is breathtaking. To begin with, you set out for the north coast, which runs below the hill on which St Anne stands. First port of call is of course the sleepy-looking harbour, which marks the start of the horseshoe-shaped bay known as *Braye Bay (page 78)*. Here you will find the finest beach on the island, which stretches as far as *Fort Albert (page 78)*, perched majestically on top of the hill. Continuing along, you pass the *War Memorial (page 70)*, which is always decorated with fresh floral tributes. The road that branches off here to the left takes you to *Château L'Etoc (page 78)*. This is the first of a sequence of fortresses standing close together along the north coast. Next comes *Corblets Bay (page 78)* with its fortress, *Fort Corblets*, followed by the ruins of *Fort Les Homeaux Florains (page 78)*, the somewhat better preserved *Fort Quesnard (page 78)* and, on the north-east corner, the remnants of *Fort Houmet Herbé (page 78)*. The view of the east coast is dominated by the fortress known as *Essex Castle (page 78)*. From its position on the edge of the cliff, it towers over idyllic *Longis Bay (page 79)*. The tiny *Ile de Raz (page 79)* in the middle of the bay is the site of yet another fortress. For the more adventurous visitor, a quite exciting and breathtaking footpath weaves its way from Essex Castle over the 100-m-high cliffs as far as the west coast – but that's better saved for another day! Your journey takes you back to St Anne, from where you can make a short trip to *Fort Clonque (page 79)*, in the bay of the same name. This is without a doubt the most important stronghold on the island and well worth a visit. It is a fine example of Victorian fortress architecture with its massive walls, ditches, battlements and machicolations, which must certainly have had a terrifying effect on its assailants. On the way back to Braye Bay, you will pass by *Fort Tourgis (page 79)*, *Fort Doyle* and, finally, *Fort Grosnez*.

Practical information

*Important addresses and useful information
for your visit to the Channel Islands*

ADMISSION CHARGES

Admission to museums and amusement parks generally costs between £3 and £4. Children are admitted for half the normal price. Senior citizens also enjoy price reductions. In Jersey, look out for the interesting *Passport Saver Ticket, which enables you to save up to 50% on admission charges to six historical monuments and sights on the island. Adults pay £10 (children £6) for admission to Jersey Museum, Elisabeth Castle, Mont Orgueil Castle, La Hougue Bie, the Occupation Tapestry Gallery* and *Hamptonne Country Life Museum.*

AMERICAN & BRITISH ENGLISH

Marco Polo travel guides are written in British English. In North America, certain terms and usages deviate from British usage. Some of the more frequently encountered examples are:
baggage for luggage, billion for milliard, cab for taxi, car rental for car hire, drugstore for chemist's, fall for autumn, first floor for groundfloor, freeway/highway for motorway, gas(oline) for petrol, railroad for railway, restroom for toilet/lavatory, streetcar for tram, subway for under-

Take the bus – it's going your way!

ground/tube, toll-free numbers for freephone numbers, trailer for caravan, trunk for boot, vacation for holiday, wait staff for waiting staff (in restaurants etc.), zip code for postal code.

BUSES

Another good way of discovering the islands is by bus. In Guernsey, for example, a one-day ticket costs £4.50, a two-day ticket £13 and a weekly ticket £29. Children travel for half-price. Tickets and timetables can be obtained on the bus itself or at the bus terminal.

CAMPING

There are camp sites on each of the islands. Unfortunately, you must leave your caravan or motor home on the mainland. You may bring your tent, but may only pitch it on an official camp site. During the high season you have to book in advance.

CONSULATES

The Channel Islands are a Dependency of the British Crown represented abroad by British Embassies.
USA
Embassy of the U.K., 3100 Massachusetts Avenue, NW, Washington, DC 20008; Tel. (202) 588 65 00; Fax (02) 588 78 70

Embassy of the United States of America, 24 Grosvenor Square, London W1A 1AE; Tel. (0171) 499 90 00

Canada

British High Commission, 80 Elgin Street, Ottawa, Ontario K1P 5K7; Tel. (613) 237 15 30; Fax (613) 237 79 80 Canadian High Commission (Immigration Division), 38 Grosvenor Street, London W1X 0AA; Tel. (0891) 61 66 44; Fax (0171) 258 65 06

CURRENCY

The pound sterling (£) is the valid currency on all the Channel Islands. Jersey and Guernsey issue their own pound notes, which are valid on all other Channel Islands – and only there. Make sure you exchange your remaining currency at the end of your holiday, before you leave the islands. It is recommended that you exchange money only at banks. Traveller's Cheques and Eurocheques up to a maximum value of £120 are accepted by all the banks. It is not possible to withdraw money from Post Office savings accounts. Credit cards are widely accepted. Unlimited amounts of foreign currency may be brought into and out of the islands without previous declaration. Bank opening times are generally as follows: *Mon–Fri 9.30 am– 3.30 pm.* These times may vary occasionally. For example, some counters are open longer in the afternoons or on Saturday mornings.

CUSTOMS

If you would like to go duty-free shopping on the Channel Islands, it is important to take into account the valid customs regulations. In this case, regulations governing non-EU countries apply, which are comparatively strict. For example, souvenirs to the value of £145 may be exported duty-free. In addition, other duty-free limits include the following: one litre of spirits, two litres of wine, 250 g of tobacco or 50 cigars or 200 cigarettes, 60 ml perfume and 250 ml of eau de toilette.

DRIVING

Driving in the Channel Islands is something of an adventure. Jersey and Guernsey boast the highest ratio of motor vehicles per capita in the world. Added to this, the roads on the islands are extremely narrow and lined with walls and hedges. Many holidaymakers have difficulty getting used to driving on the left. In the towns, there is a permanent shortage of parking spaces. If you do manage to find one, make sure you use a parking disc. The police are very diligent and check regularly to see that parking regulations are being observed. This is especially true if the legal alcohol limit has been exceeded (80 mg alcohol/100 ml of blood). Filling stations can be found in most large towns and villages. They are, however, closed on Sundays. In Jersey, the speed limit is 40 mph (64 km/h), in Guernsey 35 mph (56 km/h). In built-up areas this is reduced to a maximum of 20 mph (32 km/h) and 25 mph (40 km/h) in Jersey and Guernsey respectively. If an accident occurs, you must notify the police at the telephone number 999. It is prohibited to continue your journey until these formalities have been dealt with. Many car-rental firms on the three largest islands offer vehicles at reasonable prices (approxi-mately £105 per week, with unlimited mileage). They are marked with a red 'H' at the rear, which stands for 'hire car'.

EMERGENCIES

Police, fire brigade, ambulance and coastguard service: *Tel. 999*

HEALTH

Medical care is of a high standard. Holidaymakers must, however, pay the cost of treatment by a doctor on the spot. We therefore recommend strongly that you take out private medical insurance for the duration of your stay. Chemists are designated by a green cross outside the shop and with the words *pharmacy* or *chemist's shop*. They are open *Mon–Sat 9 am–6 pm*. Emergency services are on duty in the evenings and at weekends.

INFORMATION

Jersey
Jersey Tourism, Liberation Square, St Helier, Jersey JE1 1BB; Tel. (01534) 50 07 00, 50 08 00 (brochure line), 500 888 (accommodation reservation); Fax (01534) 50 08 99

Sark and Herm
Sark Tourism Office, Harbour Hill, Sark, Channel Islands GY9 0SB

Guernsey
Guernsey Tourist Board, PO Box 23, St Peter Port, Guernsey, Channel Islands GY1 3AN; Tel. (01481) 72 35 52; Fax (01481) 71 49 51

Alderney
States of Alderney Tourism Office, QE II Street, PO Box 1, Alderney, Channel Islands GY9 3AA; Tel. (01481) 82 37 37; Fax (01481) 82 32 45

Great Britain
Jersey Tourism, 7 Lower Grosvenor Place, London SW1W 0EN; Tel. (0171) 630 87 87; Fax (0171) 630 07 47

USA
Alice Marshall PR, 780 Madison Avenue, New York, NY 1002; Tel. (212) 861 40 31; Fax (212) 861 40 70

Canada
RMR Group Inc., Taurus House, 512 Duplex Avenue, Toronto M4R 2E3, Ontario

INTERNET

Jersey: *www.jersey.co.uk*

MEASURES & WEIGHTS

1 cm	0.39 inches
1 m	1.09 yards (3.28 feet)
1 km	0.62 miles
1 m^2	1.20 sq yards
1 ha	2.47 acres
1 km^2	0.39 sq miles
1 g	0.035 ounces
1 kg	2.21 pounds
1 British tonne	1016 kg
1 US ton	907 kg

1 litre is equivalent to 0.22 Imperial gallons and 0.26 US gallons

NEWSPAPERS

The local island newspapers, *Jersey Evening Post* and *Guernsey Evening Press*, can be bought every day in the afternoon, hot off the presses. The *Alderney Journal* appears fortnightly. In Jersey and Guernsey you can buy current editions of English newspapers on the morning of issue. Take the bus – it's going your way!

NUDISM

It is prohibited to bathe without a swimming suit on public beaches. In more secluded coves, it's possible to sunbathe topless.

OPENING HOURS

You can generally do your shopping in the larger towns and villages from *Mon to Sat 9 am to 5.30 pm.* In smaller villages and on Alderney, the shops are closed between *12.30 pm and 2.30 pm.* There are, of course, exceptions. Some shops are open, for example, on *Wednesdays* and *Saturdays only in the mornings.* The shops on Guernsey are closed on *Sundays,* on Jersey they close at *1 pm* and on Alderney at *12.30 pm.*

PASSPORT & VISA

A valid passport or identity card is sufficient for entry into the Channel Islands.

PETS

It's prohibited to bring pets with you into the Channel Islands.

POST & TELEPHONE

In largish towns and villages, the Post Offices are open on *weekdays from 9 am to 5 pm.* On Alderney they are closed over lunchtime from *12.30 pm to 1.30 pm.* Jersey, Guernsey and Alderney have their own independent postal services. On the two larger islands, the local postage stamps are valid, on Alderney, those of Guernsey are used side by side with the island's own stamps.

The most convenient way to make a telephone call from one of the yellow public telephone boxes is to use a phonecard, which you can buy at stationer's and tobacconist's shops. Local calls cost ten pence, long-distance calls cost ten pence per unit. Calls abroad are cheapest from *Mon to Fri 6 pm to 8 am and Sat/Sun round the clock.* The international dialling code for calls to the USA and Canada is 001. The dialling code for calls to the Channel Islands is 0044. Then dial 1534 for Jersey or 1481 for Guernsey, Alderney, Sark and Herm.

RADIO

Jersey and Guernsey have their own private radio stations, which broadcast round the clock on UKW frequencies 103 MHz and 104 MHz. Information relating to tourist attractions and forthcoming events are announced every day at 9.30 am and 4.30 pm. British and French stations can also be received easily on the islands.

TELEVISION

Colour televisions are standard amenities in the islands' hotels. It's possible to receive the major British television channels, which in some cases include regional news from the Islands. Hotels are equipped with satellite receivers.

TIDE TABLES

Many sights and attractions can only be reached at low tide. And because it's a safe bet that the next high tide will come – and quickly, too – it is of vital importance that you plan such excursions very carefully. It is advisable that you carry a copy of the tide tables with you at all times and that you consult them regularly. On Jersey, they are available from newsagents and on Guernsey tables are printed every day in the newspaper. Tables for the coming quarter are printed in *Alderney Magazine.*

TIME

The Channel Islands follow Greenwich Mean Time, and consequently are one hour behind Central European Time. In summer, the clocks are put forward by one hour.

TIPPING

The service staff in restaurants and taxi drivers and excursion bus drivers do appreciate a tip. A suitable amount is considered to be 10%. It is not customary to give tips to pub staff.

VOLTAGE

Voltage on the islands is 240 V AC. It is advisable to bring a three-pin adapter with flat-pin plugs.

YOUTH HOSTELS

There are no youth hostels on the Channel Islands.

WEATHER ON GUERNSEY

Seasonal averages

Daytime temperatures in °C/F

Jan	Feb	Mar	Apr	May	June	July	Aug	Sept	Oct	Nov	Dec
9/48	8/46	11/52	13/55	16/61	19/66	21/70	21/70	19/66	16/61	12/54	10/50

Night-time temperatures in °C/F

Jan	Feb	Mar	Apr	May	June	July	Aug	Sept	Oct	Nov	Dec
5/41	4/39	6/43	7/45	10/50	13/55	15/59	15/59	14/57	11/52	8/46	6/43

Sunshine: hours per day

Jan	Feb	Mar	Apr	May	June	July	Aug	Sept	Oct	Nov	Dec
2	3	5	7	8	9	8	8	6	6	3	2

Rainfall: days per month

Jan	Feb	Mar	Apr	May	June	July	Aug	Sept	Oct	Nov	Dec
14	11	9	9	9	8	9	10	11	12	12	14

Ocean temperatures in °C/F

Jan	Feb	Mar	Apr	May	June	July	Aug	Sept	Oct	Nov	Dec
10/50	9/48	9/48	9/48	11/52	13/55	15/59	16/61	16/61	15/59	13/55	11/52

Do's and don'ts

How to avoid some of the traps and pitfalls that may face the unwary traveller

Full to the brim

In high summer, the Channel Islands are full to bursting with visitors. It is above all the British who like to come to their beloved sunny islands in veritable droves. Not forgetting France, their other large neighbour, where the long summer holidays are also in July and August, as in Britain.

It is therefore strongly recommended that you book ferry tickets, hotel rooms and holiday apartments, a place for your tent and your hired car well in advance. Those who have the luxury of taking an out-of-season break, come to the Channel Islands without a second thought. And what's more, everything is cheaper in the low season!

High and low tide

The tidal range in and around the Channel Islands can measure up to 15 m. Scarcely have the receding waters pulled back to reveal sweeping sandy beaches and rocky coastlines, than the tide turns again and the foaming waves begin to claw their way back onto the shore. Don't run the risk of your quiet stroll along the foot of the cliffs turning into a panic-stricken dash for dry land. Be on the safe side and always consult the current edition of the tide tables before you set out. Every hotel has a copy to which guests can refer.

Down on the beach

The Channel Islands lie in the midst of very strong sea currents and are surrounded by dangerous rocks. Before you take a plunge into the waves, its a good idea to take time to examine the nature of the beach and the conditions in the water. Treacherous waters, sharp-edged rocks and unpredictable shallows can suddenly become life-threatening obstacles for even experienced swimmers, surfers and sailors. Make a point of enquiring at tourist offices or ask the beach patrol staff about areas along the coast where you can swim without putting yourself at risk.

Stick 'em up!

Although some years ago, the British television channel BBC decided to set a detective series in the Channel Islands, showing the entire spectrum of criminal activity, the crime rate on the islands is low in comparison with other countries. This does not mean that you can afford to be careless about your property or personal safety while on holiday. Take care not to leave valuables lying around or to flaunt them openly. Keep a close eye on identification documents, cheques and credit cards. Make sure to lock car doors when leaving your vehicle.

Road Atlas of the Channel Islands

*Please refer to back cover for an overview
of this Road Atlas*

A

Grosse Pierre
Mouissonnière
La Pointe du Gentilhomme

1
Fondu
Le Plat Houmet
The Common
Obelisk
Shell Beach

Lionaise
The Bear's Beach
Neolithic Tomb
Robert's Cross
49
St Tugual's Chapel
Shell Bay

Herm

St Peter Port
Fisherman's Beach
Harbour
Belvoir Bay
Le Manoir
Caquorobert

Prison
Rosière Steps
White House Hotel
66
Puffin Bay

Mouette
Selle Roque

Crevichon
Point Sauzebourge

2
Gavelée
67

Jethou

La Platte
Grande Fauconnière

Herm

0,5 mile
500 m

B

C

E N G L I S H

Côbo Bay

Fort Hommet

2

Fort G

Albecq

Gran

Saline Ba

3

Vazon Bay
Fort le Crocq
Fort Richmond
1,5
Golf Course
La Grande Mare
Vazon

Lihou Island

Perelle Bay
Le Trepied Dolmen
Richmond
Le Gelé
King's Mills
0,5

Priory of St Mary
Lihou Causeway
Fort Saumarez
La Rocque
Perell
0,5
0,5
0,5
0,5

Chapel of St Apolline
1,5
0,5
Mont Saint

4
Creux ès Faies Dolmen
L'Erée
Les Adams
La Houguette
Frie Baton
St Saviour Reservoir
Grantez
Les Lohiers

Rocque Poisson
La Pomare
Les Clos Landais
ST SAVIOUR
Les Jaonnets

Rocquaine Bay
2
,5
La Longue Pierre Menhir
69
Sous l'Eglise
St Saviour's Tunnel
Les Buttes

Le Douit
1,5
Le

Les Arquets
ST PIERRE DU BOIS
0,5
Les Islets
Strawberry Farm and Woodcarvers
Bird
La

Fort Grey Maritime Museum
Portelet Harbour
Silbe Nature Reserve
Les Buttes
0,5
Le Gron
1,5
Gold and Silversmith
1,5

Fort Pézeries
Table de Pions
Restored German Bunker
Les Sages
1,5
Guernsey Airport

5
73
Pleinmont
0,5
Les Nouettes
0,6
L
Ge
Me

TORTEVAL
TORTEVAL
Les Henches
Les Landes
10
3

Cliff Path
Les Simons
4,5
FOREST

6
Mont Hérault Watch House
Les Laurens
2
La Corbière
La Prévôte Watch House
Les Vil

Guernsey
Les Tielles
La Creux Mahie
La Corbière
Corbière Bay
Pointe d

0,5 mile
500 m

104

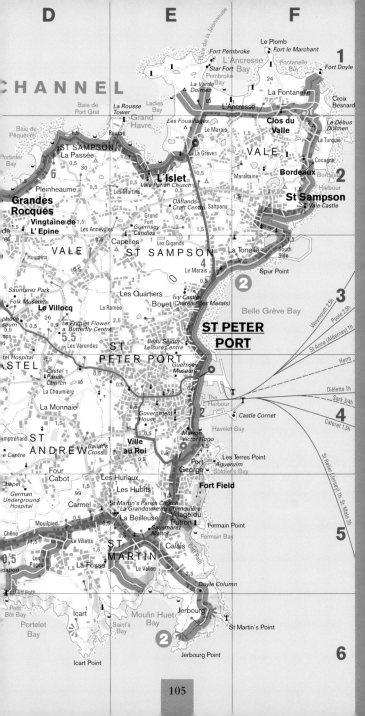

CHANNEL

1

Baie de la Jaonneuse

Le Plomb
Fort le Marchant

Fort Pembroke
L'Ancresse
Bay

Star Fort
Pembroke

Fontanelle
Bay

Fort Doyle

La Varde
Dolmen

L'Ancresse

La Fontanelle

Croix
Bésnard

Baie de
Port Grat

La Rousse
Tower

Ladies
Bay

Grand
Havre

Les Fouaillages

Clos du
Valle

Le Déhus
Dolmen

Baie de
Pequeries

Rousse

Le Marais

1,5

La Turquie

ST SAMPSON

La Passée

VALE

Cocagne

Bordeaux

Mortinfer
Bay

0,5

30

La Grève

Bordeaux

2

6

Pleinheaume

0,5

L'Islet

Maraitaine

St Sampson

Vale Parish Church

St Sampson

Vale Castle

Grandes
Rocques

Les Martins

Oatlands
Craft Centre Saltpans

1,5

Vingtaine de
L'Epine

1,5

Les Annevilles

Grand
Fort Guernsey
Candles

0,5

1,5

de

0,5

Les Gigands

La Tonelle

South
Side

VALE

Capelles

ST SAMPSON

Houmets

0,5

Les Quartiers

Le Marais

Spur Point

3

Saumarez Park
Folk Museum

La Ramée

Bouet

Ivy Castle
(Château des Marais)

Belle Grève Bay

Weymouth 2.5h

Poole 2.5h

Le Villocq

26

Le Friquet Flower
a. Butterfly Centre

2,5

St Anne (Alderney) 1h

phone
seum
0,5

0,5

0,5

0,5

5,5

Beau Séjour
Leisure Centre

Les Varendes

ST
PETER PORT

ST PETER
PORT

Herm

ASTEL

1,5

Guernsey
Museum

Diélette 1h

Castle
Parish
Church

1

Sark 3/4h

La Chaumière

Cateret 1.5h

4

La Monnaie

The
Harbour

Castle Cornet

mptréhard

1,5

Government
House

0,5

Havelet Bay

ST
ANDREW

Bailiff's
Cross

Ville
au Roi

0,5

Maison
Victor Hugo

e Centre

Four
Cabot

Les Huriaux

Fort
George

Aquarium

Les Terres Point

Soldier's Bay

St Helier (Jersey) 1h St. Malo 2h

Chapel
German
Underground
Hospital

Les Hubits

99

Fort Field

5

Carmel

St Martin's Parish Church
La Grandmère du Chimquière

Mouilpied

0,5

La Beilleuse

Village du
Putron

Fermain Point

Chêne

La Villette

Sausmarez
Manor

Fermain Bay

Les
Pages

0,5

1,5

ST
MARTIN

Calais

ation

La Fosse

Le Vallon

Cliff Path

3,5

Cliff Path

Doyle Column

Petit
Bôt Bay

Icart

Moulin Huet
Bay

Jerbourg

St Martin's Point

Portelet
Bay

Saint's
Bay

2

6

Icart Point

Jerbourg Point

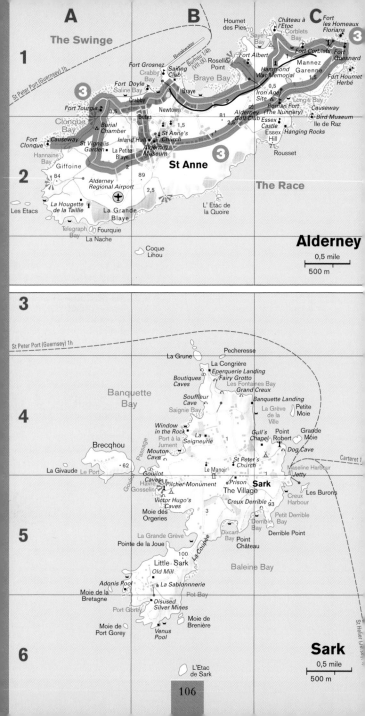

Alderney

A
The Swinge

B
Houmet des Pies

C
Château à l'Etoc
Corblets Bay
Fort les Homeaux Florians

1
St Peter Port (Guernsey) 1h
Saye Bay
Fort Albert
Breakwater
Fort Grosnez
Sailing Club
Braye Bay
Roselle Point
Hammond War Memorial
Mannez Garenne 1,5
Fort Corblets
Fort Quesnard
Fort Houmet Herbé
Fort Doyle
Saline Bay
Crabby
Braye
Newtown
0,5
Iron Age Site
Roman Fort (The Nunnery)
Longis Bay
Bird Museum
Ile de Raz
Fort Tourgis
Butes
2,5
81
Alderney Golf Club
Essex Castle
Causeway
Essex Hill
Hanging Rocks
Burial Chamber
Island Hall
St Anne's Church
Alderney Museum
Rousset

2
Fort Clonque
Clonque Bay
Causeway
St Vignalis Garden
La Petite Blaye
St Anne
Hannaine Bay
Giffoine
84
Alderney Regional Airport
89
2,5
The Race
Les Etacs
La Hougette de la Taillie
La Grande Blaye
L' Etac de la Quoire
Telegraph Bay
Fourquie
La Nache
Coque Lihou

0,5 mile
500 m

Sark

3
St Peter Port (Guernsey) 1h
Pecheresse
La Grune
La Congrière
Eperquerie Landing
Fairy Grotto
Les Fontaines Bay
Grand Creux
Boutiques Caves
Souffleur Cave
Saignie Bay
Banquette Landing
Petite Moie

4
Banquette Bay
Window in the Rock
La Seigneurie
1
Gull's Chapel
Point Robert
Grande Moie
Brecqhou
Passage
La Jument
Mouton Cave
St Peter's Church
Dog Cave
Carteret 1
La Givaude
Le Port
62
Gouliot Caves
Le Manoir
1
Maseline Harbour
Jetty
Gouliot
Havre Gosselin
Pilcher Monument
Prison
Sark
The Village
Les Burons
Creux Harbour

5
Victor Hugo's Caves
Moie des Orgeries
3
Creux Derrible
93
Petit Derrible
Derrible Bay
La Grande Grève
Dixcart Bay
Point Château
Derrible Point
Pointe de la Joue
Little Sark
100
Old Mill
La Coupée
Baleine Bay
Adonis Pool
La Sablonnerie
Moie de la Bretagne
Disused Silver Mines
Pot Bay
Moie de Brenière
Port Gorey
Venus Pool
Moie de Port Gorey

6
L'Etac de Sark
St Helier (Jersey)

0,5 mile
500 m

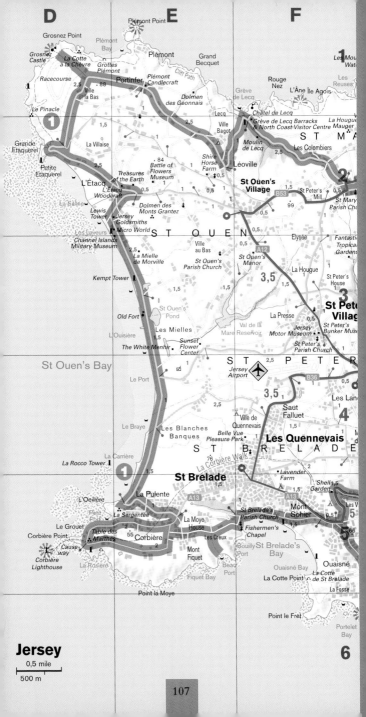

Jersey

0,5 mile

500 m

A

1
Sorel Point
La Plaine
Les Mouriers
Waterfall
Âne Île Agois
Les
Reuses
Devil's Hole
La
Falaise
La Mare
Vineyards
Barracks
Visitor Centre
La Hougue
Mauger
Les Colombiers

2
S T   M A R Y
St Peter's
Mill
St Mary's
Parish Church
St Mary's
Village
Haut
Tombette
102
Retreat
Carnation
Nursery
Butterfly Farm
and Carnation
Nursery

3
Fantastic
Tropical
Gardens
Élysée
a Hougue
St Peter's
House
L'Aleval
St Matthieu
Church
Living
Legend
Ville au Bas
St Peter's
Village
St Peter's
Bunker Museum
Jersey
useum
St Peter's
Parish Church
Panigot
Le Moulin
de Quetivel
German Military
Underground
Hospital

4
E T E R
La Fontaine
Les Landes
Mont
des Vignes
Spring
Grove
Mont
Cambrai
Bel
Royal
Mont
Felard
B36
A12
ADE
uennevais
Mont
des Vignes

5
Shell
Garden
La Haule
St Aubin
Les Vaux
St Aubin's Harbour
St Aubin's Fort
Ouaisné
Noirmont
Manor
Belcroute
Bay
La Cotte
de St Brelade
La Fosse
Portelet

6
Portelet
Bay
War Memorial
Noirmont Point
Sark 1.5h
St Peter Port 1h

B

1
Ronez Point
Lavoir
des Dames
.99
Sorel
Mourier Bay
St John's Bay
Wolf's Caves
Grand
Mourier
Perruque
Frémont
Petit
Mourier
**St John's
Village**
St John's
Parish Church
Jersey
Pearl
0,5
129
Mont Mado

2
B33
6,5
S T   J O H N
La Hougue
Boëte
1,5

St John's
Manor House
2,5
Handois
Handois
Reservoir
1,5

3
Carnation
Nursery
Jersey
Flower Centre
Retreat
Farm
**Carrefour
Selous**
A10   6
Hamptonne
Country Life Museum
Les
St Germains
Six Rues
2,5
S T   L A W R E N C E
Dannemarche
Reservoir
Trois Bois
2,5
St Lawrence
Parish Church
1,5
Ville
Emphrie

4
Millbrook
Reservoir
Mont
Cochon
Mont
Felard
1,5
Millbrook
St Matthew's
Glass Church
2,5
1,5
First Tower
Beaumont
A1
1,5

5
Ville ès
Nouaux
St Aubin's Bay
Victoria
Marine Lake
Causeway
Elizabeth Castle
L'Islet   Hermitage

6
St Malo 1h

C

1
Belle Ho
Bonne Nuit
Bay
Giffard
Bay
La Ha
des F

2
Hautes
Croix
4
A8
A9
0,5
Ville à
l'Évêque

3
Ville ès
Normans
Centre Stone
of Island
Pallot Heritage
Steam Museum
Sion
Becquet
Vincent
Surville
A9
Dannemarche
Reservoir
Sir Francis
Art G
Oa

4
75
Fliquet
S T   H E L I E
**Mont
à L'Abbé**
Vallée des Vaux

5
4,5
St Helier
Parish Church
ST HELIER
1,5
Sta
a R
Fo
Rec

6
L'Islet   Hermitage
Carteret 1h, Dielette 05h
Granville 1h

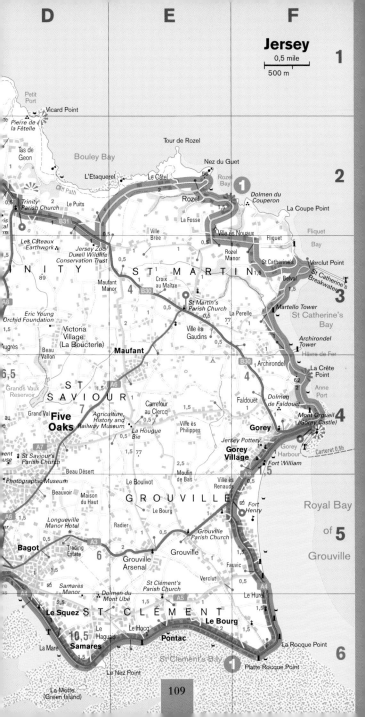

ROAD ATLAS LEGEND

Durchgangsstraße / Thoroughfare	▬▬▬▬	Route principale / Weg voor doorgaand verkeer
Wichtige Hauptstraße / Important main road	▬▬▬▬	Route de commun. importante / Belangrijke hoofdroute
Hauptstraße / Main road	▬▬▬▬	Route de communication / Hoofdroute
Sonstige Straße / Other road	▬▬▬▬	Autres routes / Overige wegen
Autofähre / Car ferry	▬▬▬●	Bac pour automobiles / Autoveer
Schifffahrtslinie / Shipping route	▬ ▬ ▬	Ligne de navigation / Scheepvaartroute
Schmalspurbahn / Narrow gauge	╌╌╌╌	Ligne à voie étroite / Smalspoor
Entfernungen in Kilometer / Distances in kilometres	10	Distances en kilometres / Afstand-kilometers
Besonders schöner Ausblick / Important panoramic view	☆ ♈	Point de vue remarquable / Mooi uitzicht
Bergspitze mit Höhenangabe in Metern / Mountain summit with height in metres	105	Pic avec cote d'altitude en mètres / Berg met hoogt in meters
Kirche / Church	⚑	Église / Kerk
Kirchenruine / Church ruin	⚐	Église en ruines / Kerkruïne
Kloster / Monastery	⚑	Monastère / Klooster
Klosterruine / Monastery ruin	⚐	Monastère en ruines / Kloosterruïne
Schloß, Burg / Palace, castle	♣	Château, château-fort / Kasteel, burcht
Schloß-, Burgruine / Palace ruin, castle ruin	⚐	Château en ruines / Kasteel- of burchtruïne
Turm / Tower	▮	Tour / Toren
Funk-, Fernsehturm / Radio-, TV-tower	📡	Tour radio, tour de télévision / Radio of T.V. mast
Leuchtturm / Lighthouse	⌁	Phare / Vuurtoren
Denkmal / Monument	⚲	Monument / Monument
Wasserfall / Waterfall	⁄	Cascade / Waterval
Höhle / Cave	⌂	Grotte / Grot
Friedhof / Cemetery	††	Cimetière / Begraafplaats
Ruinenstätte / Ruins	⸪	Ruines / Ruïne
Sonstiges Objekt / Other object	•	Autre objet / Ander object
Golfplatz / Golf-course	⛳	Terrain de golf / Golfterrein
Schwimmbad / Swimming pool	⚊	Piscine / Zwembad
Zeltplatz / Camp	⚑	Camp de passage / Kampeerterrein
Verkehrsflughafen / Airport	✈	Aéroport / Luchthaven
Regionalflughafen / Regional airport	✈	Aéroport régional / Regionaal vliegveld
Fels / Rocks	░░	Rochers / Rots
Strand / Beach	▒	Plage / Strand

INDEX

This index lists all the main places and sights mentioned in this guide. Numbers in bold indicate a main entry, italics a photograph.

What do you get for your money?

The reserve currency on the islands is the British pound sterling (£). One pound corresponds to 100 pence (p). The islands' own pound notes are equivalent to British currency. Even if the exchange rate is subject to fluctuations, and may differ from one bank to another, you can base your calculations on a ratio of 1 (£) to 1.6 (US$) or 2.4 (Can$). The high level of average earnings here has led to a corresponding level of purchasing power. Thus the Channel Islands are not the place to go if you are looking for a cheap holiday. In the high season, of course, prices are at their steepest. Outside this period, prices revert to a more reasonable level. In a standard restaurant, you can obtain a set meal for £8–£12. A la carte meals in such a restaurant would set you back approximately £10–£15. In a more elegant establishment, an à la carte dinner would cost you around £25. At the pub, a pint of beer is priced at around £1.30–£1.40. A cup of tea in a tea room is slightly cheaper, at £1.20. Museum fans must generally dig a little deeper into their pockets for an admission ticket: approximately £3–£4; children pay half the standard price. Driving a car is relatively cheap. The charge for hiring a small car for one week starts at £105 and one litre of petrol can be had for 25 pence. Bicycles can be hired for £6 per day. For a postcard to the mainland, you need a 30-pence stamp.

£	US$	Can$
1	1.62	2.38
2	3.24	4.76
3	4.86	7.14
4	6.48	9.52
5	8.10	11.90
10	16.20	23.80
20	32.40	47.60
30	48.60	71.40
40	64.80	95.20
50	81.00	119.00
60	97.20	142.80
70	113.40	166.60
80	129.60	190.40
90	145.80	214.20
100	162.00	238.00
200	324.00	476.00
300	486.00	714.00
400	648.00	952.00
500	810.00	1,190.00
750	1,215.50	1,785.50
1,000	1,620.00	2,380.00